KT-594-095

JANE GRAINING

COMPACT LIVING

MITCHELL BEAZLEY

For John Reeve

First published in Great Britain in 1999
by Mitchell Beazley, an imprint of Octopus Publishing
Group Limited, 2–4 Heron Quays, London E14 4JP

First published in paperback 2002

Copyright © Octopus Publishing Group Limited 1999
Illustration copyright © Octopus Publishing Group
Limited 1999

All rights reserved. No part of this book may be
reproduced or utilized in any form or by any means,
electronic or mechanical, including photocopying,
recording or by any information storage and
retrieval system, without prior written permission
of the publisher.

Commissioning Editor: Judith More
Executive Art Editor: Janis Utton
Project Editor: Stephen Guise
Editor: Jane Donovan
Design: Pike
Special photography: Dominic Blackmore
Illustration: The Maltings Partnership
Production: Rachel Staveley
Index: Sue Farr

ISBN 1 84000 691 9

A CIP catalogue record for this book is available from
the British Library

Typeset in Gill Sans and Univers
Printed and bound by Toppan Printing Co., (HK) Ltd
Produced in China

340258

WITHDRAWN
FROM STOCK

407249

COMPACT LIVING

CONTENTS

6	**INTRODUCTION**
12	**CASE HISTORIES**
	Solo living
	Room for two
	The compact family
	Homeworking
30	**LIVING**
	The framework
	Zoning with colour
	Creating space
50	**COOKING & EATING**
	The framework
	Storage
	Zoning with colour
	Creating space
	Display ideas
70	**SLEEPING**
	The framework
	Creating space
	Zoning with colour
	Display ideas

86	**BATHING**
	The framework
	Showers
	Baths
	Basins
	Taps
	Lavatories
	Decorating ideas
104	**WORKING**
	The framework
	Lighting
	Desk areas
114	**SOLUTIONS**
	Heating
	Lighting
	Laundry
	Overspill storage
124	Directory
126	Index
128	Acknowledgments

INTRODUCTION

A recent survey revealed that 27 per cent of the British population lives alone, the majority in cities. With the strong concomitant demand for individual living accommodation, combined with high land and property prices, space has become one of the fundamental issues in interior design today. Alongside the building of new blocks of flats with smaller living units, the conversion of period houses into flats and bedsits has been going on for years. Redundant warehouses, old factories and other industrial buildings are now divided into flats, and it is apparent that more and more single people and couples are choosing to live in studio flats in desirable districts in towns and cities rather than in two-bedroom flats way out in the suburbs.

Among architects and interior designers there is a keen awareness that space has become a luxury, and consequently a growing desire to find ever more inventive solutions to cope with space limitations. Discussions with designers on how to make the best use of a limited living area result in the same basic line of approach, time and time again: the key to small-space living is flexibility and convertibility. The trick is to increase the efficiency of a space by using it at least twice. Most of us want a place to cook and eat, living and sleeping areas, somewhere to accommodate the occasional guest, and a place to work, even if it's just somewhere to sort out the monthly bills. But each function doesn't necessarily require a separate room.

Compact living is not about creating a series of tiny rooms. Putting up walls and committing yourself to a certain size of table to produce a room for a dinner party that may happen once a month is an unaffordable luxury in a small space. It's better to have a smaller table, large enough for a couple of people, that can be extended to entertain more guests, or one that folds away to be recessed into either a wall space or a cupboard. And it's the same with spare bedrooms. In theory, it's always a good idea to have a guest room to accommodate family and friends when they come to stay, but even if the room is occupied once a month, it is still wasted space for the rest of the time. If the space is turned into a home office or maybe a workroom and is made available for other uses, but has a bed stored away on which a guest can sleep, it begins to earn its keep.

Something else to consider is the amount of space designated for circulation. Corridor and hallway space in small flats should be minimized. If the space must be retained, often to comply with fire regulations, make it dual purpose: a table that extends for parties, for example, might open out into a corridor to make better use of space.

Compact living issues are usually about the use of space on one floor and the flow between areas in what are quite often open-plan units. Considered planning, which includes giving thought to which activities merit the lion's share of the space, has to be the first priority. Then there are two main ways of tackling the space. First, keep it as open and clear as possible, and use a minimal amount of furniture so that the eye takes in the size of the space and not an excess of detail. Second, divide the space with changes in floor level and designate different areas of activity with screening walls that create the illusion of more space beyond.

Small-space living is best kept uncluttered, so to accommodate all the daily accessories that go with life, plenty of storage is essential. Hide things away where possible, but remember to keep them accessible too. Whole walls can be used for working, eating and sleeping: concealed behind doors that blend into the structure of a room, a foldaway bed will 'read' simply as wall space.

Top In this city flat, designed by Circus Architects, a corner of the living area is also used for dining. Between two red 'cupboard' doors, a glass block strip lets light filter into a bathroom under the staircase.

Centre Dual-purpose design means that when overnight guests come to stay the lightweight table and chairs move to one side and 'cupboard' doors swing open to reveal two foldaway single beds.

Bottom The owners of the flat bought a mirrored screen with a folding wooden section that is used, along with the 'cupboard' door, to partition off this sleeping space from the main living area.

Left In this tiny unit, just 40 sq m (130 sq ft) including the staircase, architects AEM created, through clever use of horizontal and vertical space, an airy living area with assigned locations for cooking, eating and seating. Behind the metal staircase – it has storage space on one side and has been converted into cupboards on the other – and below the bed platform is a bathroom. Behind this is a workroom with a bed that folds away into the wall. Limiting the use of materials in the main living area to white walls and pale wood helps to keep the space fresh, clean and open.

Above left In a 45 sq m (105 sq ft) first-floor flat in a 19th-century house, bathroom, kitchen and bedroom cupboards are arranged against a party wall in the middle of the space to create an open corridor between the living/eating/working area and the bedroom. Kitchen and study areas (cupboards that can be closed off) face into the living area; bifolding doors hide the 'kitchen' and an aluminium blind conceals the work area.

Above right Kitchen and study cupboards use the full height of the party wall to minimize visual intrusion. Architect Hugh Broughton used white walls and ceilings, with sisal matting, to enhance the light and space.

When planning the use of walls, aim to think vertically as well as horizontally. Low-level storage – units fitted under beds or seating – makes use of otherwise wasted space. An understairs space might be large enough to house a utility room or small home office; if not, it could still be used for storing awkwardly shaped items such as bicycles and other sports equipment. Use high-level spaces to hold items that are needed only occasionally and which can be accessed via lightweight ladders that fold down and store away. High-level rooms can sometimes accommodate galleries – an excellent way of adding a touch of visual drama – and these can be utilized as sleeping platforms, study areas or simply spaces for storage, acting as giant shelves while the areas below are used for other activities.

At the other end of the scale from galleries, don't neglect or forget about the 'dead' space of shallow recesses and awkward corners created (especially in period properties) by architectural features, pipework and other services. These spaces can be filled with shelves for storage or display.

As we return to some of these ideas, you will learn that 'compact living' requires considered planning, self-discipline and possibly a paring down of possessions. In those who are up to the challenge, it can prompt some marvellously inventive design solutions.

CASE HISTORIES

SOLO LIVING

In a 1930s office block near central London, converted by a property developer into domestic units of varying sizes, a busy professional woman has found an urban bolthole that suits her needs exactly.

The unit bought by the current owner was, at 70 sq m (750 sq ft), the smallest of the conversions, and the shape of the shell had already been defined. In its raw form the interior possessed all the appeal of a car park, with concrete floor, ceiling and support pillar. A red brick wall supported huge new windows and looked in onto bare pink plastered walls. Water, gas and electric supplies were capped just above the door. The industrial feel of the space, though, was very much part of the unit's appeal, offering the right framework for the simple and contemporary style of design and decoration that the owner knew she wanted.

Today's basic layout is the result of an initial collaboration with Circus Architects, and reflects the owner's desire to keep as much space as possible free for an open living area. As a PR for an international company, she entertains on a regular, albeit relatively informal, basis, hence a dining table that is large enough to seat ten comfortably and a kitchen that opens onto the living area. The service rooms – kitchen, bathroom and dressing room – are all neatly

Left A spare, minimalist approach to furnishing clearly emphasizes the flat's structural skeleton. The flank wall is divided into several neat sections, with the L-shaped kitchen on one side and a tall storage cupboard on the other. In between is the large box-shaped bathroom with the sleeping area above.

Right The worktop in the kitchen is hidden below the L-shaped bar dividing this area from the rest of the flat. Glass tiles in the walls of the bathroom allow natural light in and artificial light out.

Below left Behind the curved screen, a beech pull-up table and wall-mounted mirror (lit by strips of light bulbs) furnish this satellite of the main dressing room.

Below centre A niche in the outer side of the screen holds *objets d'art*.

Below right The spiral staircase leading to the sleeping deck is made in part of scaffolding tubes.

compacted against the flank wall, with the otherwise dead space above the bathroom ingeniously utilized as a sleeping deck. Natural light filters into the bathroom through glass block panels inset into the walls. The main space itself was barely altered, except for the addition of a curved screen in the corner. Primarily installed to comply with a building regulation, it creates a focus within the living area and at the same time conceals extra storage.

The light and spacious effect is further enhanced by the materials chosen to furnish the flat. Natural shades of pale blonde wood for kitchen units and furniture, and beech floorboards contrast subtly with the neutral cream and grey of the walls and ceilings. Huge roller blinds, which pull up from the bottom, cover the two windows, offering seclusion from the outside world while allowing daylight in.

Ground floor

Mezzanine

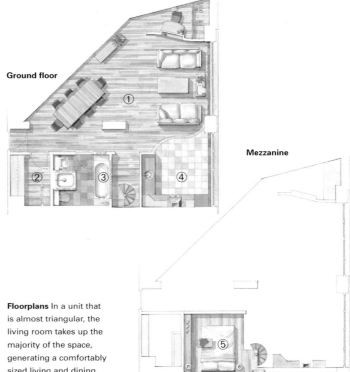

Floorplans In a unit that is almost triangular, the living room takes up the majority of the space, generating a comfortably sized living and dining area that opens out as you move from the main door to the window wall. The main service rooms – kitchen, bathroom, sleeping platform and dressing room – are to the right as you enter.

① **Living/dining area** The entrance door opens onto the dining area and table in front and to the left, with two sofas and a low table in the far corner in front of the curved screen.

② **Dressing room** This room (which holds the central heating system as well) has 3.6 m tall (12 ft) wardrobes for work clothes and shoes, and additional storage space in the cupboards above.

③ **Bathroom** On one side is the bath with storage shelves at either end; on the other are the basin, and shower that conceals the lavatory in the corner.

④ **Kitchen** This area is raised by two steps and has a cream stone floor to subtly imply its separation from the main living/dining area. Storage space has been provided in the form of wall and base units and a fridge-freezer on the back wall.

⑤ **Sleeping deck** This area holds a double bed and three double storage cupboards.

ROOM FOR TWO

West London's Notting Hill Gate is full of spacious and elegant Victorian houses that have been converted into flats and bedsits. In one of these properties a young couple, keen to live in the area, found a gloomy studio flat. Previously a rather grand billiard room, the flat had an unworkably small kitchen and an extremely cramped bathroom. The only windows looked out onto the bottom of lightwells between the adjacent buildings, so there was little light inside and no view. On the plus side, the studio extended out at the back of the house and had a large horizontal roof above. The couple felt the flat had potential, as did architects AEM, who eventually received planning permission to build an additional storey on top.

From this unpromising studio, a two-bedroom, two-bathroom flat, with a comfortably sized kitchen/diner and a light-filled living area opening out onto a small terrace has been created. The hinge between the floors is a skewed staircase that rises in a single swift flight, acting at the same time as a lightwell. This helps to disperse the gloom on the ground floor, while a generously sized entrance hall establishes an immediate sense of space. To the right of the entrance door, with a shared window overlooking the lightwell, is a pair of back-to-back bathrooms containing lavatories and washing facilities. On either side of the staircase is a double bedroom, separated by

Right In a now spacious hallway natural daylight filters down the staircase into the middle of the ground floor. During the evening upstairs lighting reflects off the ceiling into the hallway. Fluorescent fittings, which are hidden behind the horizontal overhead beam in the hall, wash light over the vaulted brickwork ceiling to help illuminate both the bedroom areas.

Floorplans In this duplex the ground floor, which is darker than the upper floor, is utilized for sleeping quarters, storage space and bathrooms. A double bathroom and the main bedroom look out onto lightwells.

① **Bedrooms** The entire end wall is filled with cupboards and is the main storage area in the flat. An etched glass wall divides the bedrooms, while the staircase wall provides an extra screen of privacy in the main bedroom.

② **Bathrooms** On one side, the bath is slotted into a cupboard-sized space looking onto the lightwell. On the other side the shower unit extends slightly into the corner of the second bedroom creating a neat space for a work table.

③ **Living area** This area possesses ample room for seating and access to the terrace through sliding glass doors. Shelves for storage and display are fitted on top of the staircase wall to accommodate a TV and hi-fi equipment.

④ **Kitchen** The staircase separates the cooking and living areas. One wall holds the oven/hob, sink and storage. A fridge and washing machine are inside cupboards on the adjoining wall.

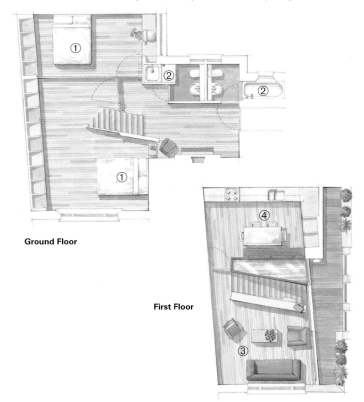

Ground Floor

First Floor

an etched glass wall to maximize light levels. The full-height timber doors to both rooms open to minimize the solid wall area.

Natural light streams through a clear glass wall into the main upper-floor living area, and sliding doors open onto a duckboard terrace, lined with plant pots. The staircase walls rise into the upper floor and good use has been made of their reverse sides. In the living area the wall becomes a storage unit that holds the TV, audio equipment and books, while bench seating runs along the kitchen side. With a sliding glass screen above and a pivoting door, this area can be divided off for cooking without losing the sense of space. Inspired use of bold colour in a neutral shell – white and brick walls, maple wood floors and lots of glass – works with the architects' spatial solutions to turn the space into a comfortably light flat.

Top left The roof light from the original studio room was recycled for the new unit in the ceiling above the kitchen.

Top centre Below the roof light on the upper level is a glass shelf, allowing light to filter down to the lower level and offering an unexpected view of the hallway.

Top right Custom-made storage forms a fixed edge to the stairwell and living area. A deep blue sofa contrasts with and balances the red staircase walls.

Left Sliding glass panels separate the kitchen from the living area.

THE COMPACT FAMILY
For a couple with a young child, a converted 19th-century schoolhouse on the outskirts of London was an opportunity to place a contemporary interior within a traditional structure. When they found it, the unit was just a shell with a small basic mezzanine. The brief to the architects, Granit, was to provide separate sleeping and bathroom facilities, while retaining the double-height open living area that so appealed to the family.

The solution involved ripping out the existing mezzanine and installing a steel structure that created two new upper levels and an open lower floor. Sweeping curves are dramatically introduced by a spiral staircase that opens onto a galleried first floor with splayed timber balustrading. Part of the first-floor void is above the hallway, suggesting height and space as you walk in. Beyond is a compact utility area hidden behind cupboard doors adjacent to the kitchen. A curved maple worktop separates the kitchen from the spacious dining/living area. The worktop curve mirrors the study balcony edge above and fits neatly around the steel structural column at one end, which is also the centre of the spiral staircase into the main attic bedroom.

A pitched roof space was opened up for the top bedroom, and the full width of the room was kept by running oak floorboards out to the apexes where floor and roof meet. Too small to hold anything

Left A patchwork of brightly coloured tiles in the kitchen creates a strong focus point and balances the impact of the curved timber balustrading on the galleried landing above. Natural materials in the framework of the building, such as the yellow brick walls and the oak floor, harmonize with the stainless steel structure that dominates the core of the flat.

substantial, the expanse of open floor appears spacious. A curved wall leads to a circular bathroom with cylindrical shower and walk-in dressing room/cupboard. On the mid-level, the child's bedroom is just 2m (7ft) high, with doors opening onto the balcony and the double-height void of the dining area below. Here, the edge of the sloping roof is concealed by a window seat, and deep cupboards extend to full ceiling height. Opposite, steps lead down into a bathroom to make use of reduced headroom below. At the far end of this level is the open part of the galleried floor with office space.

The materials used give a coordinated look. New and old oak floors, ash doors, exposed yellow brick, timber with stainless steel and a bold selection of ceramic tiles fuse the space, filling it with interesting detail, but maintaining a feeling of openness.

Above A neat utility cupboard, on the left as you enter, has a double sink with shelving above and washing machine and tumble dryer stacked to one side.

Far right The ceiling above the ground floor seating area creates an intimate retreat within the open plan living space.

Right The ash-faced cupboard doors to ceiling level suggest height in the child's bedroom. A window seat disguises the slope of the roof.

Floorplans A triple-height unit has been converted for family living, retaining an open space that uses all of the available floor area at ground level. The staircase defines the hallway, while a worktop divides the kitchen from the living and dining area. Light enters the lower floor via an open area above the hallway and a double-height void above the dining space. The first floor houses a child's bedroom, a bathroom and a galleried study. On the upper level the main bedroom is beneath a pitched roof. A circular bathroom sits behind the staircase top. The dressing room is on one side of the bathroom and there is a cupboard on the other. Doors lead onto a terrace.

① **Hallway** The front door opens onto the hallway, which features plenty of cupboard space.

② **Living/dining area** The dining table occupies the double-height section. Light floods in from the open floor above and from two large windows and French doors in the wall at the front of the building. Seating is under the mezzanine.

③ **Utility cupboard and kitchen** To the left of the entrance is the utility cupboard, beside which is a kitchen space with room for a cooker surrounded by floor and wall cupboards. The sink and dishwasher are in base units; there is a fridge below the worktop.

④ **Bedroom** The child's room has spacious built-in storage cupboards and plenty of floor space.

⑤ **Bathroom** A porthole window in this bathroom looks onto the hallway.

⑥ **Study/home office** As one of the couple is a student, a work area was an essential space.

⑦ **Bedroom and bathroom** A walk-in dressing room/cupboard adjoining the bathroom means that a sleigh bed is all the furniture needed in the main bedroom.

⑧ **Terrace** Double doors lead out onto a wooden decked terrace.

Ground floor

First floor

Attic floor

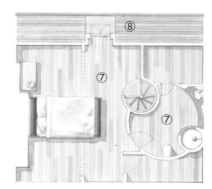

Right The storage wall in the living/working space is designed to function on one side as an office, with desk, drawer and shelf space; a sliding shutter door pulls down to conceal everything. To the left is the fireplace, as well as the TV, video and audio equipment and accessories – neatly stacked in boxes and drawers. To the left of the wall is the aisle leading to the bedroom and to the right is the entrance hall with mezzanine storage space above.

HOMEWORKING

In the last decade developers have taken enthusiastically to converting redundant industrial buildings for domestic use, and these transformations form the backbone of new residential property in London. The Piper Building, decorated with mural panels by artist John Piper for British Gas in the early 1960s, is just such a development. For one successful businessman, whose work involves a great deal of foreign travel, it offered the opportunity to mould from scratch a base in which he could live and work.

Architects Wells Mackerath were asked to design the 145 sq m (1560 sq ft) unit. They removed the mezzanine that ran the full length of the space as their client would be spending work and social time at home and they wanted to retain some double-height space to make the flat as airy as possible. A fitted kitchen wall was installed at one end of the flat, with overhead cupboards extending well above the height of conventional kitchen units. In the middle of the flat is a spare bedroom with a cross-storage wall on either side, the more central of which divides the living/working area from the sleeping/bathing area. The entrance hall stands to one side, with a narrow side aisle on the opposite side. Access to all the high storage cupboards and the mezzanine storage space created over the entrance hall was achieved by fitting a continuous stainless-steel bar

Left The architects designed this table for their client. An artfully engineered two-part structure, it has a black walnut veneered top and a metal section gateleg support on castors. Folded out, the table is spacious enough for meetings or to seat up to ten for dinner parties.

Main picture Custom-built in MDF and stainless steel, the fitted kitchen wall was painted a sharp shade of lilac to provide a colourful contrast to all the white and shades of grey. Floor-to-ceiling cupboards at one end are accessed by the portable, lightweight ladder.

Far right The home office desk and shelves are simply and quickly concealed by a sliding shutter that looks like a wall surface.

Right The entrance hall is under the mezzanine, with hanging space for clothes and room below for boots and shoes. Boxes provide room for bags, briefcases and a fax machine, and help limit desk clutter.

at a fixed height around the perimeter of the living/dining area and kitchen. A lightweight ladder is simply moved around as necessary. A mezzanine was installed over the main bedroom, and this holds the main bathroom (cleverly hidden from the bedroom) and a sleeping platform/storage space. Under the mezzanine are a walk-in dressing room/cupboard, a bathroom/utility room and the entrance hall.

Ingenious detail abounds in the design of the fittings throughout the flat. Everything slides, glides, pushes or pulls so that the many cupboards and storage units appear to be wall space. Sliding shutters pull down to hide the desk, lightweight panels screen off windows and a push-and-tilt panel conceals the TV. For someone who works from home and often has business clients around for meetings, the flat presents a perfectly professional appearance, but everything is effortlessly and neatly tucked away out of sight once work is over.

Mezzanine

Ground floor

Floorplans The flat was redesigned to include a mezzanine at the sleeping and bathing end, which left the living/dining area with the full double-height space.

① **Main bedroom** In one corner is a large walk-in cupboard with hanging space one side and storage on the other.

② **Bathroom/utility room and entrance hall** These are fitted into the space beneath the mezzanine. Laundry equipment is kept out of sight in the bathroom/utility room.

③ **Spare bedroom** Full-height pivotal glass doors close the spare bedroom from the main bedroom and living/dining area.

④ **Living/dining area** Slate-grey sofas separate the kitchen/dining end of the area from the multifunctional storage wall on the opposite side.

⑤ **Kitchen** Fitted base units hold the dishwasher and oven.

⑥ **Mezzanine** A galleried bathroom has a bath sunk into a raised dais – so that it is hidden from the main bedroom – at one end and a shower at the other. On the other side of a divide is a sleeping platform/storage space.

CORK CITY LIBRARY

LIVING

THE FRAMEWORK

The living room is where working people spend most of their time at home. In many households it has taken over from the kitchen as the hub and core of the home; it is a room of both activity and relaxation. For most of us, it is a place to retreat from the stresses and strains of the outside world, where you can curl up on the sofa with a book or a magazine, lounge against a pile of cushions to watch television, or listen to a new CD. It's where you sit and talk with your partner, children or friends, and it should be somewhere you feel completely at ease. However, the living room is also likely to be the most public room in your home, a place where you entertain guests and endeavour to make them feel welcome and comfortable. It's the face or image that you present to the outside world: a statement of your personal style.

As well as being somewhere to relax, in a small home, where the kitchen is not big enough to accommodate a table, the living room will double up as a dining area, and the table in turn may also be used as a desk or hobbies' table. Because it may be called upon to fulfil a variety of functions, the living room becomes a very complex room to organize and furnish. It is extraordinary, then, that whereas no one would even contemplate designing a bathroom or kitchen without drawing up a scaled plan first, we have a much more haphazard

Above A small one-storey glassworks in London's Docklands was converted by architects Hawkins Brown into a two-bedroom house with a third bedroom/study.

Right The living/dining area of the converted glassworks makes good use of the full height of the building. A wall and ceiling of glass maximize the openness so that the room is flooded with natural light, whatever the weather outside. The sculptural staircase creates interesting shapes and corners in the room, with space for a seating unit along one wall. Around the other side of the staircase, a neat square has been cut into the wall and this is used as a serving hatch between the kitchen and the dining area.

Left Designed to combine one- and two-storey living, the main living area in this converted glassworks is beneath the lower end of a shallow sloping roof on the river-side of the building. The smaller rooms and service areas – kitchen, bathrooms and the bedrooms/study – are neatly stacked on two levels at the front of the house overlooking the street. Angular roof space, clean architectural detail and a wall of stairs with a galleried landing define the living area, while open doorways on both levels allow light to filter into the main space.

approach to designing our living rooms. Not surprisingly, it makes good sense to get out the graph paper and plot the area, marking in permanent features such as the windows, doors and fireplaces, and traffic flows to other rooms. In the living room, where electrical equipment is almost always essential, planning the location of power points is important too. As well as television, video and audio equipment, it is quite likely that a variety of localized lighting will be needed for specific tasks, such as reading.

Once the fixed elements of the area have been drawn in, the key to making the living room work is getting the seating and storage elements right. If there is room, a good basis for seating is an arrangement of a couple of comfortable sofas – two-seaters are much more useful and ergonomic than single armchairs or three-seater sofas (people don't like sitting in rows in social situations). And try to provide half a dozen dining chairs that can double as occasional chairs when entertaining friends. Most of us watch some television in the living area, even if there are sets in other rooms, so the seating must be arranged to enable comfortable viewing. Seating also needs to facilitate conversation (we tend to turn our bodies towards people as we talk and no one enjoys shouting across distances). Seats for solitary occupations, such as reading, also need to be considered.

Right Circus Architects
were asked to convert
an awkwardly shaped
double-height shell into
a flat with living/dining
area, kitchen, bedroom
(and room for overnight
guests), work area and
two bathrooms. The brief
stipulated maximum
flexibility in the use of
the space. The kitchen (to
the right of the picture)
is raised by one step to
separate it from the main
living area. Beyond the
seating is a dining area
with two foldaway single
beds. A bathroom, study
area, dressing room
and bedroom, with a
glass panel that opens
onto the double height
of the main space, are
on the mezzanine level.
The second bathroom is
under the stairs.

One space-saving option in open-plan units is to store electrical equipment, accessories and books on freestanding open shelving that can also act as a space divider. In small rooms, even though the cost is likely to be considerably more, electrical equipment and the accompanying paraphernalia is usually much better concealed and stored on shelves and in drawers behind cupboard doors, along with the boxes of games, piles of glossy magazines, catalogues and other bits and pieces that are part of our daily lives. Keeping all of this clutter behind closed doors wherever possible helps to maintain an overall impression of clean space, openness and calm.

It is difficult, however, to imagine a living area without any books and pictures, and, if you want your home to appear larger than it is and to feel light and airy, a disciplined approach to display is a priority. If you find it impossible to live in a space without some personal belongings on view, then try to look for less obvious places to locate them. For example, fit shelves to hold books or *objets d'art* high up on walls above doors or windows, and don't overlook the invaluable display space that is to be found around and between windows. Group those items chosen for display and limit them to interesting arrangements in carefully selected areas to help to maintain an uncluttered appearance.

ZONING WITH COLOUR

It is generally accepted that daytime rooms look best when decorated in pale, light tones, which help to keep them as airy and spacious as possible. At night, on the other hand, bolder, richer colours are more responsive to the glow of electric light and make for a warmer, more welcoming ambience. If your living area is small and is used in the day as well as in the evening, heavy colours on walls are not recommended as they would make it seem even more restricted. This does not mean that achieving an intimate and friendly atmosphere is ruled out altogether – it can still be accomplished with clever lighting. Nor should you outlaw strong colour altogether in your home. Instead, think of using it in blocks, rather than across whole areas. Employing clean white tones or soothing neutral shades of cream, grey or beige to decorate a basic shell means that even small areas of strong colour will have a striking prominence. However, the overall impression of spaciousness will be maintained.

Just as you can use screens and walls of cupboards to divide up areas within a room, so colour can be used to delineate space. When these two devices are put together, they work very successfully. Particularly when a flat only comprises one main room, colour can help to partition off visually areas set aside for different functions –

Far left Architects Littman Goddard Hogarth used assertive oranges and yellows to make a bold impact in a tiny flat. Used on moving screen doors and the small enclosed spaces, these colours are completely surrounded by a white ceiling and matching walls. With pale wood floors, the space is not overwhelmed.

Left The bright orange door slides back to reveal the bedroom and cover a translucent glass panel that allows borrowed light from the living area to filter through into the internal bathroom. This not only opens up the bedroom area, it also ensures more privacy in the bathroom. Checked orange and yellow bed-linen helps to establish a visual link between the different areas.

for example, the working corner, the cooking/eating space, and the area for sleeping or watching television. To achieve different zones in a room, you don't need to restrict colour to large blocks of vertical space, such as screens, walls or cupboards. The upholstery fabrics chosen for sofas and seating units can trigger off the same visual effect and make a seating area appear slightly separate from the rest of the room.

Quite often, monochromatic schemes are still the first choice in small flats, but without using strong variations in colour, it is still possible to achieve a similar, but more subtle, effect by using texture to add visual depth and to mark out functional territory. Grainy wooden floorboards, chalky matt paintwork, crisp smooth linen and knobbly woollen *bouclé* are all rich, natural textures that make an interesting contrast to the more raw appeal of concrete, stone, stainless steel and shiny, reflective paint surfaces.

The use of pattern in small spaces needs to be rationed. Pattern tends to demand most of the attention in a room and eats up visual space quite greedily. Instead of introducing pattern through wall finishes, textiles or carpets, consider collections of small, contained accessories, such as groups of black-and-white photographs, a shelf of books, or even a single row of identical drinking glasses.

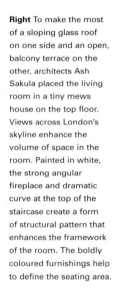

Right To make the most of a sloping glass roof on one side and an open, balcony terrace on the other, architects Ash Sakula placed the living room in a tiny mews house on the top floor. Views across London's skyline enhance the volume of space in the room. Painted in white, the strong angular fireplace and dramatic curve at the top of the staircase create a form of structural pattern that enhances the framework of the room. The boldly coloured furnishings help to define the seating area.

Right A small flat above commercial premises was converted by architects Granit, who removed the ceiling and pitched a glazed roof behind the existing parapet. This allowed a mezzanine level for a bedroom and bathroom to be added and created a greater sense of space and light in the main living area.

Below The open design of the new wooden staircase allows light to flood in from the glass roof down the stairway to the entrance door. The reinforced front wall is used extensively for storage (bookshelves also act as an extra sound and insulation barrier).

CREATING SPACE
Improving the spatial quality of your living area is about illusion: making the space appear larger than it really is. This effect can be achieved in a variety of ways, although they are grouped here in three quite different categories: redecoration, reorganization and lighting. Redecoration is the most basic and easily achieved technique, as well as being the least expensive. It can lighten and brighten up a room, making it appear more spacious.

Improving the organization of a room so that there is sufficient storage to allow a place for everything brings a clean, uncluttered visual order and efficiency to the room, making it calming to live with. It helps enormously when you are creating space in a living area if you take an imaginative approach – for example, by planning ways to incorporate storage into the fabric and framework of a room, instead of introducing extra items of furniture.

If this is not an option, when buying furniture look for pieces with dual-purpose potential. Trunks and blanket chests double up as storage spaces or low tables to hold magazines and coffee cups, and if you place a cushion on top, they may even be used as occasional seats. In period properties, where windows project, the classic approach to making optimum use of the space is to build a low cupboard with a seat cushion on top. Today an enormous range of

Below The owner of this flat has a large collection of CDs to house. Storage space was designed to fit unobtrusively below the wooden ledge on top of the staircase wall, where it would still be easily accessible.

sofas and day-beds – for sitting and sleeping – is available, as well as upholstered footstools with bed mechanisms folded inside. Smaller items, such as stools that convert into steps to access high storage space, are also worth investigating.

Structural changes require more commitment, both financially and imaginatively. However, sometimes quite small and relatively straightforward changes, such as removing a partition wall to open up internal views and reshape the living area, result in the most startling improvements. Where a generous amount of ceiling height is available, the addition of a gallery or mezzanine offers an exciting and dramatic change. It can alter the volume of space, as well as increasing the floor area, to give you at least one other useful 'room' that could be designated for, say, a home office.

At the top of many buildings, roof space offers an equally dramatic and wide choice of spatial options. If the area is opened up by removing the ceiling, adding skylights or even a glazed roof, the space can be transformed to become inspiringly alive and light-filled. In a city a panoramic view over an eclectic collection of rooftops can have a dramatic appeal to rival the softness of a country landscape. Few of us have the confidence (or the essential building knowledge) to make structural alterations without professional help. While

Left Fashion designer Ben de Lisi discussed storage ideas for his London flat with his interior designer, Adam Dolle, during the initial stages of planning. Dolle suggested building cavity walls in the sitting room, ostensibly to create interest and shape in what was a plain, square room lacking any architectural features, but also to hide service pipes and wiring, and to enable shelving for books and magazines to be neatly recessed into the walls.

Right In de Lisi's flat a freestanding wall, built in American walnut, serves to separate the sitting room from the tiny kitchen beyond. It was designed to allow light from the kitchen windows to flood the entire space. The room is furnished with classic sculptural shapes that are contained and precise, leaving clean, open space all around them.

simple, internal partition walls or basic gallery structures do not usually require planning permission, it is likely that any extension or attic conversion will require the necessary official approval, and there will also be fire regulations to comply with. If in doubt, always seek advice first.

In houses and flats where structural change is not an option and the living area has limitations – a low ceiling, for example – opening up the room in an attempt to make it airy and spacious may not be the right answer. A helpful alternative is to break up the space with a screen or dividing panel that does not reach the full height of the room. A screen allows you to define boundaries without fitting doors. By sectioning off an area – for eating or cooking, say – with a partition that allows light to filter over and through from above, and positioning the screened-off area at the furthest point from entry into the room, the space is given a focal point. Screening also gives the impression that there is a similar volume of space on the other side of the partition.

Partitions can be inexpensive ways to divide up space. They may be used either to section off an area for a specific function, or to hide things away in lieu of cupboards. Partitions can be made from panels of MDF or chipboard, hinged together and given a coat of paint;

Left Architects AEM increased the volume of utilizable space in this flat by removing the ceiling and roof trusses, and supporting the roof pitches on new steelwork. To the right of the stairs is the bathroom and a small office/storage room/spare bedroom. At the top is a bed platform. Beyond the stairs and kitchen units lies the dining space and a seating area.

Right The main living area in the same tiny flat is divided and defined by the angular shape of a hit-and-miss staircase. Doors were added to the shapes and spaces created by the treads on one side of the stairs to turn them into useful storage space. On the other side of the stairs, kitchen units fit neatly under the framework.

Left Built-in cupboard space, if it is a viable option, is ideal. It can be integrated into the room space and painted or finished to work with the existing styles and materials. Here, audio equipment stacks neatly behind a door that pulls up and slots into the cupboard when access is needed. Immediately below is a set of drawers with sections for CDs and cassettes. Some electrical equipment, such as this slim-line hi-fi unit, complete with speakers, is so smart and attractive that it is unnecessary to hide it away, while wall-mounting saves valuable surface space.

this is within the abilities of even the most unenthusiastic DIY-er. Although sandblasted glass, set into full-height frames anchored to floor and ceiling, requires installation by an experienced fitter, it is another excellent way of creating a visual barrier. The real advantage in this case is that borrowed light filters through the whole area of the screen from the space beyond.

If you plan out the lighting at the same time as the layout of the room, it is easier to achieve the right balance between an option for privacy and a sense of spaciousness in a multifunctional living space. A general level of background, ambient lighting supplied from a source such as downlighters, mounted or recessed into the ceiling, will light up corners of the room without making shadows and will create an illusion of greater space. This form of lighting is all that is necessary for moving around the room, having conversations and watching television. Writing, reading and working at a computer all require localized task lighting, which is more easily supplied by table, desk and floor lamps. It also makes sense to invest in dimmer switches to provide maximum flexibility and control of light, allowing subtle mood changes in a room, from cool brightness to a soft warm glow (dimmer switches can be wired to overhead fittings and to the electrical circuit for lamps).

Right The ultimate in discretion, this television is sleekly unobtrusive, recessed into the wall space, with all of its unattractive 'workings' and wiring concealed at the back.

COOKING & EATING

THE FRAMEWORK
Above all a kitchen is a functional room, primarily a place where meals are prepared and cooked. For many of us though, food is much more than just a source of energy, and cooking is an enjoyable part of everyday life, rather than a tedious chore. If you spend much time in the kitchen, once you have planned out how to make the space operate as efficiently as possible, style, comfort and ambience will all be very important considerations. At the other end of the scale, if you seldom cook or eat at home, creating a conventional kitchen will be a waste of time and money. This is even more relevant where space is at a premium.

In this case, a better solution is to organize a neat little worktop area to accommodate necessities – a sink, hob, refrigerator and maybe a microwave oven – that can be tucked away behind a screen in the corner of your living area, or possibly behind a cupboard door in a hallway or corridor.

If kitchens are required to operate on a higher culinary level than simply warming through a croissant or pouring boiling water into the cafetière, a little more thought is necessary. The basic plan in all working kitchens, whatever their size, is that the three essentials – sink, cooking facilities and refrigerator – need to be within about a double arm's-span reach of each other to form a triangle.

Left Storage units with fitted castors are incredibly versatile. In this tiny attic kitchen, the units pull out for easy access to the contents and give extra worktop space. They can be wheeled to different areas and slide neatly away after use. Here, every inch of vertical space is utilized for storage, with a rack for wine bottles suspended from the eaves and a metal bar to hold utensils fitted under the window frame.

Above Wooden storage units form a jigsaw of different shapes that use every bit of wall space and look good open or closed. Larder units are behind the centre panels with appliances ranged either side.

Below A central cube-shaped dining 'room' was designed by architects Littman Goddard Hogarth to fit in the middle of the main living area. A table folds away to resemble a sculpture.

Below right The hinged tabletop unclips from its wall slot and can be opened out to half-size.

Right When extended, there is room for six at the table and use is made of corridor and overspill from kitchen space. The chairs are easily stacked when not in use.

Worktop and storage space are positioned between the triangle points, providing a range of surfaces to prepare and put things on, and cupboards, drawers, shelves, racks, and so on to store ingredients and hold cooking pots, pans and utensils.

Before you venture out to choose units and equipment, it makes sense to examine the way in which you live and what you really need, and to design your kitchen accordingly. For someone who works all day, has no time to shop for anything other than essentials during the week and cooks most evenings for one or two people at the most, good storage facilities for food, including a spacious refrigerator, freezer and larder, are main priorities. People who love to cook and

entertain, have friends dropping in for meals on a regular (if casual) basis and are able to shop daily have different requirements. They need more workspace, plus plenty of storage room for pots, pans, serving dishes and crockery, as well as adequate cupboard space for food. These people probably feel happier with a friend or two around to chat with them in the kitchen, so avoiding the sense of cooking in isolation while everyone else is enjoying drinks before the meal. If the kitchen has room for a table and chairs, this is not a problem (it is convenient, where possible, to have a dining area in the kitchen in any event, as, with the demise of the formal dining space, eating takes place in the kitchen much of the time anyway).

With the opportunity to start from scratch, you may decide to go completely open-plan, combining living/eating and cooking space, or you might want to combine living and sleeping in one room, so that the kitchen is large enough to cook, eat and entertain in. If there is just enough room for essentials and big structural changes are not an option, look at ways of opening up the kitchen to the living area. If the kitchen leads off a corridor, would double doors (or no door at all) make the room appear more accessible and rather less isolated? Alternatively (and an idea that seems to be back in favour again), is it possible to install a serving hatch?

STORAGE

A run of unbroken kitchen units, with no intrusive knobs or dials, has a clean streamlined appearance. Everything is hidden away and efficiently stored, so the overall impression is one of spaciousness. In the kitchen, built-in units have even more validity than in other areas of the home. They can conceal all your appliances so that they too resemble cupboards, and today's manufacturers produce furniture containing every type of drawer, basket, shelf and rack to pull, slide or fold out. There is something calming about having everything in its place, which is also a compensation for the loss of the traditional kitchen ambience. Tiny kitchens, however, especially the classic galley shape where counters run along parallel walls, or U-shaped kitchens where three walls are utilized, are not suited to banks of fitted cupboards because the framework and doors take up too much space. There is also the argument that fitted cupboards seem clinical and cold.

Ask yourself, then, do you want to have everything hidden away? If you eat and entertain in the kitchen, the atmosphere should be welcoming. After all, the kitchen is a place where the senses very much come alive. Smell, touch, taste and sight all have their role to play in preparing, cooking and serving food. A pile of terracotta bowls brought home from a Spanish holiday, wooden spoons in a basket

Above On a raised dais in the corner of the main living area of this two-storey flat, designed by Circus Architects, fitted wall and base kitchen units are defined by bright red doors. A dwarf wall, with a black granite worktop that is also a breakfast bar, combines with the raised level and colour zoning to separate this area visually from the rest of the room.

Right When the cupboard doors are closed, this kitchen wall appears to be a block of strong vital colour with a stainless-steel box in the centre. A range of different cooking appliances, including a microwave fitted in the space directly above the main oven, are all neatly hidden away behind the doors to give a stylish, uncluttered feeling.

Left This ground-floor
kitchen fits under a
sloping wall created by a
staircase. Originally one
long narrow room, dining
and cooking areas are
now separated by a
dividing wall. A large
square doorway and tall
open window slots allow
natural light into the
room from the dining
space beyond. The fitted
area is contained beneath
a beech worktop and
white appliances sit
alongside white-painted
cupboard doors. A large
collection of stainless-
steel pots and pans and
a rail of utensils gathered
together over the years,
are all accessible and a
pleasure to look at.

bought in a Provençal street market, well-worn bread boards discovered
in junk shops, and racks holding *batterie de cuisine* assembled over the
years, are all evocative objects that you may not wish to hide away. On
the other hand, despite their charm, unstructured kitchens have few
labour-saving qualities and would probably irritate a busy person living in
a small space. A compromise, retaining an unstructured or semi-
unstructured look without losing the built-in organization of a modern
kitchen, is probably the best option in this case.

Floorstanding units, installed along the kitchen walls to hold
appliances, gadgets, equipment, some food storage and the sink will
give you all the efficiency you need. Open shelves and racks fitted
above work surfaces allow you to stack items that you find attractive
but also use regularly, so there is no time for dust to gather. Here,
you can introduce colour and style. Display rustic plates and bowls in
rich, vivid shades of ochre, jade green and indigo blue, or a row of
plain, elegant white plates or jugs beside a stack of stainless-steel
saucepans, a stoneware pestle and mortar, or a line of cookbooks. It
makes sense, and saves time and effort too, to have useful equipment
and utensils ready to hand and visible, yet stored above work-surface
level so that preparation space does not become cluttered.

Below A collection of
much-loved china, glass,
crockery and silver adds
rich warmth when
grouped in cupboard
shelves on the wall at the
dining end of the kitchen.

ZONING WITH COLOUR

However much we enjoy cooking, few of us think of the kitchen as a place where we can go to relax. It's an active, doing type of room, albeit active and doing at different speeds. At the beginning of the day we want it to be a bright, breezy, upbeat place; challenging the brain to wake up as we make the coffee, squeeze the oranges for juice, toast the bread and digest the daily news. Preparing an evening meal still calls for a clean, efficient, workmanlike environment, but with more mood and ambience. At this time of day a glass of wine and a plate of olives is set on the worktop beside you as you cook the tagliatelle, toss the salad and discuss the day with your friends or partner.

White is the colour that represents clean efficiency and, as with all small rooms, decorating with white enhances the feeling of spaciousness. The kitchen interiors illustrated in this book reflect the current vogue of relying on white to create an illusion of space by using it all over the framework, walls, ceiling, skirting, window frames, and so on. Blocks of bright colour are then introduced on unit cupboard doors and other furniture. Tuscan burnt orange, bright acid yellow and indigo blue feature widely, as do red and black, the traditional lacquer colours. These are all confident colours that can hold their own against each other, as well as the strong, angular

Right The owners of this London flat decided on bright lacquer colours, red and black, to create a bold, upbeat statement in this minute kitchen/dining room. Designed by the architects, Granit, a curved work bar butts out from the wall to form the main work surface and hold the hob. The space underneath contains the oven, crockery and saucepans. Every inch of vertical space is fitted with shelves, racks and hooks for storage.

Far right Cupboards on either side of the window are painted red to draw them into the colour scheme. The cupboards, which also hold the TV, are deep enough to give space for a window seat. On the near wall, open shelves carry interesting objects to shift attention from the radiator below. The chequered floor and red-painted areas make this room appear very colourful; the majority of the space is, in fact, white.

shape and structure of the contemporary kitchen. Colour defines and delineates space and, in this room, where the activities of cooking and eating may often take place simultaneously, they can help to separate the cooking/working zone from the eating/relaxing zone. Fitting boldly coloured floorstanding units with open shelving above is less intrusive than fitting matching wall-mounted cupboards, because the strong colour is below eye level, but it still balances out all the detailing of accessories above the work surface.

An interesting development in kitchen design is the practice of combining contemporary hardwearing materials, such as stainless steel and brushed aluminium, with their traditional, hardy counterparts of stone, granite, slate and marble. All of these materials make for excellent surfaces that will withstand the daily round of water, grease and sharp knives. Their naturally handsome appearance changes to take on the character of whatever they are teamed with, be it intense bursts of chic, jazzy colour or cool and classic light-coloured wood. Different materials used for counter tops and splashbacks help to separate different areas used for different purposes. The materials mentioned above are good choices for the surfaces on which most of the work will be done; sealed, waxed or stained wood is suitable everywhere else in the cooking/eating area.

Left Tuscan burnt orange effectively 'zones' this one-wall kitchen and breakfast bar/worktop from the rest of the living area, in a flat designed by Wells Mackereth. Painted MDF cupboard and drawer fronts, stainless-steel splashbacks (into which power points and taps are recessed) and concrete worktops have been combined to produce a contemporary, streamlined and colourful place to cook and eat.

Right Bright colour is used in a rustic, yet stylish way to achieve simplicity and warmth in a very small country cottage. Bands of chalky yellow and blue contrast gently with lots of natural wood. The table base, which is also painted blue, blends in and is not too visually obtrusive in this deliberately and lovingly unstructured kitchen/dining area designed by The Works.

CREATING SPACE
Once you have decided on an all- or semi-fitted kitchen and on keeping the framework of the room pale (or white), the kitchen can be further streamlined by the efficient organization of storage. However, before you try to find the right storage fittings, study your kitchen paraphernalia. Be ruthless and get rid of gadgets, crockery and anything else that is never used.

Work out what you really need. Is it really essential to have one set of china and glass for everyday use and another for entertaining? Crockery can be just as versatile as dual-purpose furniture. Look for bowls that work equally well for puddings and salads, and for attractive and functional dishes that can be used in the oven and freezer and on the table.

Storage units that slide out on tracks tend to be more useful in tight spaces – pulled out, you can see exactly what you have. They can be fitted with baskets, trays and shelves to hold everything, from cereal boxes to saucepans. Units fitted with castors enable you to pull them around for easy access and they can be moved to different parts of the kitchen as needed. If you are stuck with conventional doors and shelves, customize them to suit your needs – for example, by removing the central shelves and replacing them with sets of baskets on runners. Keep work surfaces clear, but hang a rail at splashback height for utensils. If you can sacrifice some worktop depth, have wall cupboards that come down to meet it to hold bulky items that are awkward to haul up from floor units (if possible, create worksurfaces to slide out from under the original spaces). Consider appliances such as dishwashers in compact or slimline versions, and small ovens that can be built into wall or base units.

Far left Separate eating areas are not usually an option in small homes. In this kitchen, just enough space to hold a table and chairs has been created. Visual space and light is 'borrowed' from the open corridor beyond.

Left A tall, thin room converted into a kitchen, with one wall devoted to cooking/ storage space, economically utilizes a high vertical wall area. Natural light pours in over the work surface and sink.

Above The main living area is divided from the cooking/eating space by a half-glazed wall. Kitchen and built-in seating units around the table are pushed into the corners to use up all of the space.

DISPLAY IDEAS

Kitchen paraphernalia looks wonderful on display – when it is done with a touch of imagination. Items with real character, such as glass kilner jars filled with brown sugar, plump sultanas or different types of pasta or rice, look attractive and wholesome when set in neat, straight rows together. Mixing bowls and thick Tuscan pottery, stacked Leaning Tower of Pisa-fashion, have an equally appealing, random charm of their own. Discrimination is an important watchword when you decide exactly what to put on open shelves – half-used tubes of tomato purée and open bags of flour just don't have quite the same aesthetic quality. Fill open shelves immediately above worktops with attractive items that are used regularly (but make sure that food is not placed directly above steamy areas, such as sinks and hobs).

Alternatively, a not quite so accessible shelf fitted directly above a window or a doorway could be used to hold a special collection of jugs or platters that are only used occasionally. Window space used for shelves generally goes against the principle (and natural instinct) of always allowing as much light into a room as possible. When space is at a premium, though, and the view is less than good, a row of shiny saucepans outlined against the sky can be worth the compromise. Open-grid metal racks are great forms of shelving. Easy to fit, they

Above The combination of stainless-steel saucepans, frying pans and colanders on wooden shelves is both attractive and practical. Fluorescent lights, fitted under lower shelves, illuminate the worktops below.

Left Shutting out natural light is normally anathema to architects. In this situation, however, where storage space is extremely tight, the view uninspiring and another source of natural light is available, open shelves have been fitted. They help to give a sense of balance to the long run of floorstanding kitchen units underneath and distract attention from the fact that the two windows are not the same size.

have a contemporary, industrial appeal that works well with a minimalist or traditional style of decorating. In addition, they have the advantage of allowing the light to come through, which is especially important when they are positioned over workspace. Hanging racks are equally good. When suspended from the ceiling and made from different types of metal and wood (or combinations of the two), they make use of the vertical space directly above your head and turn storage into a versatile, changeable art form. Open metal baskets, full of colourful vegetables such as peppers, and hooks holding strings of onions, bundles of fragrant herbs and garlands of red chillies suspended in the air, alongside metal whisks, sieves and cooking pans, turn a workroom into a proper kitchen and make good use of otherwise wasted space.

Other forms of storage, such as metal or wooden plate racks, also work well as practical, yet decorative, display devices. A plate rack fitted above the sink removes the need for a draining board. When the rack is fitted above a hob or cooker, plates and serving dishes are kept warm and accessible. Shaker-style peg rails work in the same way when used to display *batterie de cuisine*, so that often-used equipment is readily accessible and also forms an interesting decorative focus.

Left Open metal shelving above the stainless-steel worktop in this kitchen is designed so that items can be stacked on top, slotted into place or hung from it. Once washed, plates and glasses can be left to drain there to avoid worktop clutter.

Top If you need to use window space for shelving, the open metal variety has the advantage of letting as much light through as possible.

Bottom An old storage shelf, painted the same colour as the walls, holds a treasured collection of *batterie de cuisine*, with strings of chillies and garlic heads conveniently positioned on the wall next to the oven and hob. A metallic knifeholder fits into the space below.

SLEEPING

THE FRAMEWORK
For some people the bedroom is a peaceful haven, a calm retreat and a place of sanctuary at the end of the day. For others it's a waste of valuable space. Certainly, when space is at a premium, devoting a large chunk of it to an area unused during daylight hours might seem recklessly indulgent. On the positive side, bedrooms can often take up 'awkward' space that is difficult and impractical to use for purposes other than sleeping. The eaves in attic rooms are a good example of this, having traditionally served as interesting and neat spaces for the horizontal attributes of the bed. Rooms with limited access to natural light — those facing into the well of a block of flats, basements and even ground-floor rooms looking onto city streets — are ideal for bedrooms. So long as you can live without feeling the sun on your face when you wake up, and can bear having the bedroom below, rather than above, the place where you live, cook and eat, these rooms can be the perfect choice.

In many small homes a bedroom needs to play a dual-purpose role. It might have to double up as a study or an office, if you work from home. The bedroom might even be part of the main living area in a very small flat or, in a family home, an alternative space for listening to music, watching television or using a computer. In these

Above In this London flat, designed by Littman Goddard Hogarth, a small room off the living area serves as both a spare bedroom and an office. A panel, painted the same colour as the wall, has been fitted to the bottom of a folding double bed in order to screen it from sight when not in use.

Centre At the head of the bed a hinge mechanism makes pulling the bed out a simple operation. Fitted straps span the mattress to hold bedding in place.

Right When it has been pulled down, the bed is just as comfortable as a conventional version. Recessed into the cupboards, which create a convenient side table, the head of the bed is comfortably enclosed. A sliding etched glass door on the far side of the room ensures privacy but allows light through.

Right This studio is one-room living in grand style. The simple open staircase leads to a high-level sleeping deck with plenty of space for bed linen and so on in a custom-made platform that extends the length of the deck. Below is a tiny kitchen and shower room, concealed behind white cotton screens. Other features, such as the ornate black marble fireplace, high wing-back chair and circular dining table, lend a generous sense of scale. Neutral tones created by using natural materials for furnishings and flooring make the space appear clean and uncluttered.

instances, where having a bed in full view isn't conducive to the other activities that take place in the room, there are various options. Beds that fold down from the wall are space-saving and convenient: the bed effectively 'disappears', folding away complete with bedding, and can be disguised to become simply part of the wall. It can be neatly hidden away behind various types of screen, such as sliding doors or Venetian blinds, and storage facilities – shelves, cupboards, drawers and hanging space – can be ranged around the bed area to make use of the whole wall. The main advantage of this type of bed, as opposed to a sofa bed or a futon, is that it can be quickly put away in the morning and pulled out at night – completely made-up and ready to use. Another plus is that the floor space occupied for sleeping can be used for other purposes once the bed is put away. Any furniture used in that floor space should be lightweight and easy to move, or on castors, so that it does not become an obstacle late at night when you are tired, or in the morning when you are in a hurry.

Another option is a sleeping platform, bed deck or gallery, where the bed does not completely disappear from view, but is moved up onto a higher plane. Adding another level to a room in this way is aesthetically pleasing and makes a wonderfully dramatic impact, whether the style be minimalist, contemporary or traditionally grand.

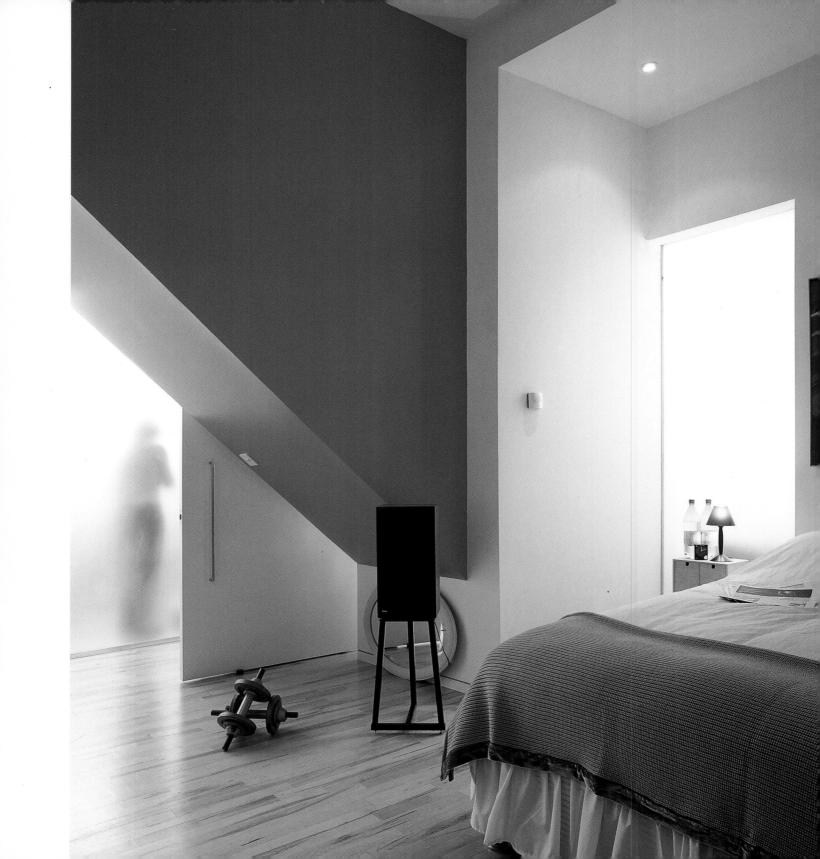

Where ceiling heights are generous and there is room for a large mezzanine or gallery, there will space below to create an enclosed room, such as a bathroom, or an open seating area that would be lent a sense of comfort and intimacy by the lower ceiling. Even in rooms where the ceilings are not so lofty, there may be enough room to create an agreeably snug sleeping platform with plenty of space for bookshelves or cupboards underneath.

Major structural changes – a new mezzanine level for example – require professional advice. On the other hand, a bed platform with storage below may be achieved with your own design input and the help of a capable joiner (always check that the floor can bear the load first). Stairs providing access to the bed may be just as theatrically visual as the platform itself, and can play an exciting sculptural role in the dynamics of a room, especially in open-plan units. Spiral staircases are a prime example, and they use up only a small amount of floor space in comparison with conventional staircases.

Whether your bed is on a platform in an open-plan unit or in a dedicated room, it is clearly the main consideration when furnishing a bedroom, closely followed by storage requirements. Single beds are easy to plan around: they look neat and angular up against walls or centred under windows. Double or king-size beds, on the other

Left A lower ground-floor bedroom borrows light from other areas in the flat through etched-glass wall panels. Solid colour separates the staircase from the bedroom and forms a sculptural screen between bed and door.

Above In a tiny bedroom the bed sits against the low wall space under the dormer window, with storage below accessible via side and end panels. The bed-linen provides a bold block of colour in an otherwise neutral shell.

hand, are more likely to take up most of the floor space in small bedrooms and become the main focal point. As the majority of time spent in a bedroom is likely to be taken up in using the bed, shortage of space shouldn't necessarily be a problem. In fact it may even enhance the feeling of comfort and intimacy. Once you have come to terms with the fact that your bed may fill the room, you could just go with the idea and opt for something that will dwarf the room, but express your personal style – a splendid antique bed in carved mahogany or polished brass, for example, or the simple, bold, structural good looks of a modern four-poster.

Bedroom storage – the other essential – has to be carefully planned (the potential for untidiness in this room is considerable, and clutter makes small spaces seem even smaller). Clothes, shoes and accessories all need to be hung and stacked so that they can be stored and retrieved easily. Built-in cupboards that hide everything neatly away behind closed doors that slide, rather than open out, are the best option in very confined areas, leaving clean space after the bed has taken pride of place. And if there is no room for even this type of storage, consider the argument that dressing in a bedroom is a convention, rather than a necessity: it might make sense to put up hanging space elsewhere in your home.

Far left In the stylish and
contemporary bedroom
of a city flat, Circus
Architects have designed
a low-level bed that
seems to float above the
floor. Low-level shelving
on either side of the bed
(more storage is provided
in the adjoining dressing
room and bathroom
areas) and clean white
walls and bed-linen pull
the eye towards the focal
point: the fabulous skyline
beyond the window.

Left Structural pillars are
both a full-height bedhead
and the framework for
an opening etched-glass
panel. Controlled by
hydro-pneumatic gas
springs, it opens over the
double-height living area,
adding to the spectacular
view from the bedroom.
When closed, the glass
allows borrowed light
to filter through from the
space beyond.

CREATING SPACE

The very fact that a bed takes up so much space can be used to advantage, if you utilize the areas around and beneath it properly. Divan-bed bases with storage facilities are widely available; storage is usually in the form of shallow drawers that slide out and is mostly suitable for folded clothes or bed-linen. If space is really confined and you need to make use of the whole drawer, measure how far it extends and check that other furniture in the room will not impede access.

A platform built under a mattress may inspire you to create custom-made storage to suit your own needs. You could use boxes with racks inside for storing shoes, shelves to hold piles of shirts and drawers for underwear and accessories. Spaces at the head and foot of a bed can also be useful storage areas. Instead of using bedside tables to hold a lamp, book and glass of water, choose an item that doubles up as storage, such as a chest of drawers or a small trunk.

Another option is to make a bedhead with a shelf area on top that extends beyond the width of the bed, while wall-mounted furniture, lighting or shelving – which still allows you to see the area underneath – creates the illusion of space. Mirrors, when applied to all or part of a wall or cupboard doors, work cleverly both to extend space and to amplify the light.

Left An attic master bedroom suite in a three-storey flat, designed by Granit, is accessed from a spiral staircase. The curved line is repeated at the top of the stairs and in the curved wall surrounding a circular shower room underneath the roof pitch. A storage cupboard below the sloping roof is angled to blend in with the shape.

Below The full width of the bedroom is kept by running oak floorboards into the apexes where floor and roof meet. The bedhead wall extends out on either side to hold reading lights. A sleigh-bed is the only piece of furniture to take up the valuable floor space.

ZONING WITH COLOUR

For some of us the bedroom is about relaxation: the atmosphere needs to be soft, sensual and gently tranquil. Others require a bright, crisply clean wake-up look. Whatever your temperament, there are a couple of points to consider before making a decision. For most of us, the bedroom is used in the bright natural light of morning and the soft artificial light of evening – study your chosen colour at both ends of the day. Certain colours, such as greens and yellows, can change character quite considerably in warm artificial light. Fashionable orange, for example, can overheat and be uncomfortably strong in a small space. If you want to make the room appear as spacious as possible, use white, neutrals or shades of the same pale to mid-tone colour (mix varying quantities of white with the darkest tone chosen) on all surfaces. Walls, flooring, curtains or blinds, bed-linen and features such as radiators, all coloured in the same or similar tones, create fewer of the visual breakpoints that can disrupt a room.

Alternatively, if you wish to make a feature out of the intimacy of the space, dark jewel-like colours will intensify the atmosphere. Remember too that colour can draw attention to a particular area, enliven a room devoid of architectural features, or simply distract from an unattractive view.

Right Fashion designer Ben de Lisi has effectively colour-zoned his tiny bedroom and bathroom space using rich earthy tones of neutral colours with white and black. White lifts the ceiling and, combined with a black-and-glass screen wall, it separates the bathing area from the bedroom.

Far right A mirrored wall reflects light from the ceiling and the putty-coloured carpet on the floor exaggerates the impression of space. From this angle, custom-built storage cubes take on a double dimension too. The bedhead has floor-to-ceiling cupboards on either side, plus a place to mount bedside wall lights and recessed, neat shelving space.

DISPLAY IDEAS

For those who truly are meticulously tidy, bedroom storage affords the opportunity to play with interesting forms of display. The neat symmetry of jackets, trousers, skirts and dresses hanging smartly in a line, shelves stacked with piles of crisply pressed shirts and rows of shoes in the space beneath create a whole wall of pattern and colour in a room. And try clustering other elements that you wish to have on show together to create a stronger impact. Books, paintings, photograph frames and collections of smaller items all make bolder statements when grouped together, providing a room with a focal point. Objects displayed in open shelving, fitted with mirrors in the wall behind, will seem more defined and distinct.

Instead of using up floor space, use walls and, in particular, higher spaces for decorative storage. The tops of cupboards are excellent places to display larger items and sculpturally strong shapes such as vases, jars, old leather suitcases and interesting boxes, including those of the circular hat variety (which also make useful storage). Narrow shelves fitted at picture-rail, above-shoulder or head-height, again displaying sculptural or simple circular shapes, lift the level of focus and extend the height of the room. The key to exaggerating space is to keep the room clean and uncluttered; if this is not in your nature, it's better to admit it and hide everything away.

Left Not intimidated by lack of space in this small bedroom, the owner has used a framework of neutral tones and white to create a spacious setting and filled it with large pieces of furniture and interesting features. An imposing marble fireplace, which has been decorated with paintings and candlesticks, creates a strong focal point.

Below left A cluster of photograph frames draws the eye to the window and the light and space beyond. The depth of the window sill is extended by shelf space created from a boxed-in radiator. A large abstract oil painting in the corridor leading to the bedroom is paler in tone than the wall below, making the area appear taller.

BATHING

THE FRAMEWORK

When it comes to the bathroom, it is generally accepted that space is somewhat restricted. This is the room that is often considered last and which frequently gets squeezed into a windowless area too small for any other use. Bathroom layouts need to be carefully planned, not just to ensure that everything fits in, but also to allow comfortable access to fittings. To help you with this, manufacturers of bathroom furniture often supply catalogues with printed grids and cut-out shapes to represent the fixtures. If the room is very small, it can be similar to putting a jigsaw together: only one combination will work. The least expensive and simplest option is to place fittings as close to the relevant water supply or soil outlet as possible. However, saving money on pipework can be a false economy if it means alterations later on.

Bathroom designers often complain that traditional pedestal fittings, which are floor-anchored, waste space. Wall-hung versions make small bathrooms seem larger and they can be hung at the height to suit you. Wall-mounted taps can be space-savers too.

Where space is restricted, quirky colour schemes, overbearing in larger spaces, can be indulged, as can more expensive materials. The surfaces in very small bathrooms must be water-resistant, but this should not inhibit your choice of style.

Far left White ceramic tiles, clean and fresh, are a practical space-enhancing choice. The wall-mounted basin is semi-inset into a tiled shelf that extends under the opaque glass block window, keeping the line of the wall unobtrusive.

Left The cistern and all the pipework for this WC have been neatly boxed in. False panelling, with a useful shelf on top, is covered in the same tiles as the wall. Pale all-over colour schemes always help to give a spacious feel to a room.

Right This shower room and WC – designed by Wells Mackereth – manifests clean space in every sense. Recessed sections hold toilet rolls on one side of the room and a mirror on the other. Fittings to operate the shower and WC are also recessed, as are the light fittings that illuminate the area. Sliding etched-glass doors allow light to filter through, and a network of putty-coloured mosaic tiles makes the room appear chic and spacious.

Below This shower room has one wall of fixed glass panels and another fitted with sliding doors for easy access and lots of light. Aquamarine mosaics create a watery mood; recessed fittings give a streamlined look.

Right In a bathroom that receives natural light, glass bricks were used for the walls and a shower cubicle. Large areas of mirror and cream mosaic tiles help to maintain the sense of space and light in this room.

SHOWERS

Exhilarating and energizing, the shower does more than simply cleanse. If there's no room for a bath of any size, a shower can always be created by lining the walls and floor of a room with tiles and fitting a drainage hole. Alternatively, low-profile shower trays with drainage holes can be partly recessed into the floor. Positioned for easy access behind etched-glass or glass-brick screens, they are less claustrophobic because of the filtered light (and screens, of course, protect the other fittings from the water). Heating pipes set under the floor tiles will keep the shower warm and dry.

If you have space for an enclosed shower, you can design your own screening doors. Glass (the toughened safety variety) is the obvious material; alternatively, think about etched-glass or glass-brick panels. If your shower is a tiled alcove, the 'door' can simply be a shower curtain on a rail. Shower doors, available hinged or pivoted, can be reversed to hang on either side. Sliding doors, consisting of two or more panels that overlap when opened, are space-savers, and concertina-style sliding doors are another option. Shower trays are made of steel, fireclay and composite materials (usually the most economical) in a range of sizes and shapes. Corner versions are designed in a triangular shape to fit into the space (shower enclosure doors and panels are available to fit around them).

Far left In this minuscule
bathroom the architects
have managed to create
enough space for a bath,
which slots neatly into
a cupboard-sized space.
Taps are recessed into the
tiled wall on one side and
a marble shelf under the
window faces onto the
lightwell of the building.

Left Another 'illusion'
is achieved by sinking
a bath into the floor
or a platform. In this
bathroom mezzanine the
bath has been sunk into
a stepped dais so that it
effectively disappears.
Beneath the balustrading,
a walnut bench seat lifts
up to reveal storage
space for towels, toilet
rolls, and so on.

BATHS
For some people a shower's stimulating effects will never replace the ritual of bathing, and they will go to great lengths to install a bath in the smallest of bathrooms. Of course, it's always been possible to position shower heads and fittings at one end for a dual-purpose bath (shower fittings on taps are useful for washing hair but not the same as 'real' showers), but today there are baths specially designed for showering. These have a wider section at the 'shower end' of the bath, and the same end runs straight down, rather than sloping, to meet the bottom of the bath at a right angle, so that you can move right to the end. In a small bathroom, where there is not enough space for a separate shower and bath, this is probably the best compromise.

Shower screens that extend the whole length of the bath to limit splashing are available. Standard baths measure around 1.7 m x 71 cm (5.8 ft x 28 in) and require their own widths again in floor space to ensure room to manoeuvre comfortably. Most bathroom furniture manufacturers have baths in several different sizes and these can be as small as 1 sq m (1.2 sq yd) . However, unless it is fairly deep, such a bath would be very unsatisfactory to use (water lapping just above waist height is a novelty in a foreign hotel, but at the end of a working day it would not make for a relaxing soak).

BASINS

BASINS A vast choice of shapes and sizes of hand basin is available, but in a small bathroom, where a pedestal fitting will simply use up valuable floor space and create unhygienic nooks and crannies, a basin that cantilevers off the wall is a better option. Very small versions, designed for use in cloakrooms, tuck into corners or recess into walls but are only really suitable for washing hands. However, there are ranges of good-sized basins designed for corner spaces, with room on the shelf at the back for standard taps. Innovative creations can be purchased from designers such as Philippe Starck, who has produced basins that possess modest outer dimensions and generous 'counter' spaces at the back to hold toiletries and make-up. Wall-mounted basins have a number of advantages: they can be set at a height to suit your household and they have syphon covers to conceal pipes and waste traps available in finishes to match your taps, which are more aesthetically pleasing than conventional plastic versions. Alternatively, semi-inset basins (the back fits into a piece of furniture or a shelf projecting from the wall) or inset basins with over- or under-bowls are available. The latter can be housed in cupboards with space for spare toiletries and cleaning materials. Although a boxed-in basin takes up extra visual and 'real' space, it may provide enough storage to make the loss worthwhile.

Above Pipework is concealed behind painted timber panels. Taps and a water spout are mounted onto the wall above the inset bowl to leave the surrounding area free. There is useful cupboard space directly below the bowl for storage.

Right An arrow-slit window of stained glass allows light from a hallway to illuminate a stainless-steel basin. Shelving 'wings' and a towel rail underneath make clever use of a restricted space.

Below Tight in the corner, this basin is inset into a very small, floorstanding cupboard and has just enough room on top for taps and water beakers. When not in use it is hidden behind a folding storage door.

Above A smooth bowl of stainless steel, set below an oval panel of taps and water spout, has an almost clinical appeal that works well in small spaces. The heated towel rail swings out into the room for easy access.

Above On this corner basin, with inset bowl, small but elegant three-hole chrome mixer taps have two separate valves that mix the water just before it leaves the central spout.

Left A mono-bloc tap with a tall spout fitted into the surround at the side of the basin makes optimum use of space. The mirror-fronted wall cupboard has accessible open shelving. Below, double doors conceal valuable storage space.

Below The sense of space is enhanced by walls of mirrored cupboards, and by neat cubby holes for shelves and display space in stone-coloured mosaic-tiled walls that accentuate the contours of the wall-mounted basin and taps.

TAPS Baths and basins are available with or without pre-drilled tap holes, which enables you to have plumbing and taps mounted into the wall above, or into the surround. This frees up the area where the tap fittings would usually be (and makes it easier to clean). It also allows you to fix taps in the middle rather than at the end of a bath, saving valuable space. It may enable you to enclose the bath in an alcove, with ceiling-height cupboards at either end, or keep both ends free for open shelving. Innovative technology has also created clean-lined fittings that totally conceal plumbing works, increasing visual space.

When taps are smaller than average, and set into the wall or surfaces around baths or basins, they merge with their surroundings, creating a streamlined effect. Monobloc mixer taps, for basins or baths in compact single-lever designs, take up less space than conventional pillar taps and often include pop-up wastes. The ultimate in streamlined tap design is Philippe Starck's hand pump '10010': with its gently curved handle it is the archetypal single-lever mixer. Concealed single-lever wall-fitting bath mixers are wonderfully neat and contained, just a circle of chrome on a surface.

If everything else is hidden from sight – for example, in a completely tiled shower room – taps will be the most conspicuous items on show, so choose the best quality fittings that you can afford.

LAVATORIES

Old-fashioned high-level WCs, where cistern and pan are separated by a pipe, are not a sensible choice for a small bathroom. It makes sense to try to contain the fittings in as small an area as possible to free up vertical space for storage, or for opening out the room with mirrors and panels of translucent glass that allow light in. You could use either a traditional wash-down or a modern syphonic cistern: there is no appreciable difference in size, although the latter is quieter and more efficient.

Back-to-wall lavatories, where you can conceal a separate plastic cistern behind a false wall, will save space. Bear in mind that the top of the concealed cistern needs to be a minimum of 80 cm (31 in) above floor level to flush successfully. The necessary false wall can often be used to recess other fittings such as basins, bidets and wall-mounted towel rails. Building a false wall creates a useful shelf area above the fittings, where bathroom accessories can be stored.

Boxing in the cistern allows you to have enclosed storage space, as useful cupboards or rows of shelving may then be recessed into the joinery. Close-coupled WCs incorporate the cistern and pan so they are reasonably contained. However, the height is preordained and, because they have pedestal pans, valuable floor space is used up and interrupted.

Above A curved false wall runs around the bath and under the window. This continues onto the adjoining wall to allow the WC and semi-inset basin to be wall-mounted, leaving the floor space free and creating a useful storage shelf.

Below A glass brick panel lets in light from the next room, illuminating the smart and practical colour scheme created by setting white walls against blue mosaic tiles. The boxed-in cupboard conceals plumbing.

Above Even in very small bathrooms corners can be used to make the most of space. Here, a wedge-shaped box, with mosaic tiling and a lid of slate that allows easy access to the plumbing, is used to cover the cistern.

Right A wall-mounted WC and basin are set on a false wall that holds a deep recessed shelf on top with a mirrored wall above. It also conceals plumbing for the shower and wall-mounted taps. The red panel to the right is a pivoting door.

DECORATING IDEAS

Images suggested by water and bathing offer a wealth of interesting visual, textural and sensual ideas for bathroom accessories. Add touches such as shells ranged along window sills, pieces of coral stacked on shelves alongside piles of clean towels and flannels, and baskets of ivory coloured soaps mixed in with pebbles from the beach, for example. With just enough room for fittings, though, where do you display accessories in a small bathroom? If you decide to recess and wall-mount fittings such as WCs and basins, shelving space can be created immediately above. Alternatively, if you carry on a false wall to ceiling height, recessed shelves may be fitted. If you set a bath into a mosaic-tiled surround, you can make a shelf around it or, if a bath fits neatly between walls, there may be room for display shelves at either end. Anything wall-mounted – radiators, towel rails, accessory holders – saves space, as do ingenious shower curtains with pockets for toiletries and soaps. Towel ladders that fix or lean against walls save space and add a contemporary look.

Reflective finishes – shiny chrome and stainless steel – combined with silk emulsion paints bounce light off walls and enlarge the sense of space. Larger mirrors and light colours on all of the surfaces also help. And valuable space can be gained by rehanging the bathroom door so that it swings outwards instead of into the bathroom.

Far left Tongue-and-groove panelling is good for boxing in walls and fittings in a bathroom. Here, the area at the back of the bath conceals the plumbing. A recessed box, lined and fitted with glass shelves, carries a neatly labelled collection of seashore treasures. The area is illuminated by a light fitted into the top of the display box.

Left In this bathroom intelligent use has been made of the angled space below a large staircase. A built-in cupboard holds washing appliances and, at the end of the bath, the owner has used the slightly enclosed wall area to hold rows of open display shelves.

Above Neat cubby holes make excellent storage and display spaces. Built into false walls, they integrate more smoothly and are far less conspicuous than wall-mounted racks and holders for various bathroom accessories.

WORKING

THE FRAMEWORK
New technology – desktop computers, the Internet, E-mail and fax machines – means that more and more people are now able to work from home. Combined with changes in employment, which have led to a greater number of people becoming self-employed and carrying out freelance work, there is a greater need for home offices than ever before.

However desirable it may seem to have a separate work room, a place to shut the door on at the end of the day without needing to clear everything away; often in a small home this is simply not viable. It is much more likely that your work area will be part of a dual-function space. If your home office is to be used for sorting out domestic paperwork and bills, and simply requires a table, chair and a couple of box files, then there may be room in the hallway, on a landing, or under the stairs. Alternatively, there may be a corner of the kitchen with room for a wall-mounted 'shelf' table and stool.

If you require a more professional space, the first area to consider is usually the bedroom, which is generally unused during the day. Try to plan the space so that each function is as self-contained as possible. If the arrangement is intended to be long term, you will be best served by a bed that folds away, completely out of sight. Sleeping and working require such different attitudes of mind that if you are

Left A small study area in a flat shared by a couple who do not work from home is hidden when not in use by a perforated aluminium blind that drops from a recessed slot in the top of the framework.

Right When the blind is raised there is plenty of worktop space for paperwork, as well as for reference books in the shelving cubes above, and audio equipment and CDs below. Clearance space has been allowed so that the chair can be placed under the worktop when the blind is lowered.

reminded of one while attempting the other, it won't help you relax or concentrate. If you can't fold the bed away, at least try to screen it off from the rest of the room. It is equally important to keep the work area – desk, computer, telephone and files – out of sight when you are unwinding at the end of the day and preparing to go to sleep. Again, screening the area will help, but purpose-designed space that can be completely closed off is definitely the best answer. A working 'wall', with space at the bottom for a chair and a work surface, surrounded by storage cubes, drawers and shelves, is ideal. Fit doors that concertina, slide or simply open and close when the working day finishes. The same arrangement would work just as well in the living room, where the activities that take place are not so at odds with each other as in the bedroom.

It's important to remember that working from home requires a different approach and frame of mind. Normally, the change to work mode is triggered when you leave home and set out for your place of employment. When you work from home this no longer applies, so most people will find that it really helps to create a well-organized area where you can go to 'switch on'. A whole range of attractive filing and storage systems are widely available to help you to make the most of your work space.

Far left Clever design turns what would usually be wasted space on this attic bedroom wall into a desk that can be folded away when not in use. There is plenty of storage too, in the cupboards ranged on either side under the eaves, which are clad in white-painted boarding. Using the same neutral tones everywhere in rooms such as this one helps to minimize the irregularity of the shape.

Left On the mezzanine floor of a city apartment the balcony guarding becomes the framework for a small study desk. A metal shelving trolley is all the storage needed by a businessman who only occasionally works from home and limits his office equipment to a lap-top computer and a telephone.

LIGHTING

Natural daylight is best for illuminating areas used during the day. Place your desk or table near a window if possible, to help energize, encourage and enthuse flagging thought processes. It is important to remember, though, that computer screens should not be placed in front of, or facing onto, windows or other light sources, as an uncomfortable glare might occur.

For workspaces without natural light, and for those times when artificial light is also required, an overall ambient light supplemented by strong direct adjustable lighting that can be positioned on the worktop is needed. Anglepoise lamps are ideal. Designed to comply with the principle of form following function, the head and classic cantilevered structure can be manoeuvred to shine in any direction. Current versions may be used with halogen bulbs to give a sharper and cleaner, more workmanlike light than the tungsten alternative. If space is really at a premium, there are versions of Anglepoise and other desk lamps designed on similar lines that clip onto the sides or backs of worktops or shelves. Floor lamps can be useful task lighting too; there are designs available that twist, rotate and extend as required. If your only source of light is a central fitting, extend the cable and fit a hook in the ceiling above the work table to avoid the shadows caused when the light shines from behind you.

Left A landing in a London house has floor-to-ceiling bookshelves on one side and a desktop housing a computer and printer on the other. During the day light streams in through the two adjacent windows. By night an Anglepoise lamp illuminates the desk space.

Right A work area in the corner of a living room has a fabulous chrome floor lamp, which can be positioned directly over a computer keyboard.

Far right In this tiny office, created out of a vault under a pavement, the architects introduced several ingenious ideas into the space, including a clever way of making a virtue out of the lighting cable. It snakes across the sloping ceiling to hang above the desk.

DESK AREAS
One of the advantages of working from home is that you have the freedom to decide on the furniture, accessories and colours that will surround you. When choosing a desk, table or worktop to be used on a daily basis, there are several guidelines worth considering.

Sitting at a table for hours on end places pressure on the spine, so it is important to have the right chair. Chairs that fold down, such as director's chairs, are ideal in small spaces. If you have enough room, investigate office chairs, which are designed to support the back properly. They should be comfortable and allow your feet to rest on the floor with your knees slightly below hip level. Desktops are easy and inexpensive to improvise with MDF cut to size and painted. They can be wall-mounted to flip out and away as required. Alternatively, place them on trestle legs or a pair of filing cabinets. They should be high enough to allow your legs to fit underneath when your hands rest on the worktop and your elbows are bent at a 90-degree angle.

Where a home office is very much part of the living space, good organization and storage are not only efficient, they prevent the area from spreading and intruding into the rest of the room. Make sure that there is a place for everything, even if you just use a collection of baskets with tie-on labels for different bits of paperwork.

Far left A custom-built work space for a home-based businessman has shelves over the worktop for folders, reference books and papers used frequently; drawers under the worktop store extra stationery. General lighting is recessed in the top of the framework, with a small adjustable lamp for added flexibility. When the work is over a door slides down to hide the space from view.

Left In the corner of a busy family kitchen a 'shelf desk' is at the heart of the day-to-day running of the household and is a place to compile shopping lists. Diary and telephone are at the ready on the worktop, with a useful pinboard above. A set of shelves fitted over the worktop holds telephone directories, magazines and cookery books.

SOLUTIONS

HEATING

If you live in one big room or in a small-scale house or flat, standard forms of central heating and radiators can be problematic: in open-plan flats conventional radiators on outer walls rarely supply efficient heating; in small rooms radiators eat up valuable wall space. Underfloor heating distributes warmth across whole rooms to maintain an even temperature throughout your home, and if you choose stone, ceramic or wooden floors, it is a particularly worthwhile investment. Whether you choose a wet or dry system, it needs to be installed professionally.

If you decide to stick with radiators, there are plenty of designs to choose from. Reproductions of classic cast-iron radiators are available in tubular steel and can be bought in small sections. Convector radiators are a compact alternative: they take up less space than conventional radiators and can be hung at any height on walls. Another real advantage of convector radiators is that they can also be recessed into trenches in floors or fitted into plinths, the latter being particularly suited to bathrooms – in bath surrounds – and kitchens – in kitchen unit bases. Small and very discreet, they make good use of otherwise dead space, including skirting boards. Tube radiators, ideal for the angles where floors and sloping ceilings meet, are stylish and space-saving floor-mounted versions.

Far left The small alcove in an entrance hall is just large enough for this classically designed tubular steel radiator. They are made to order in different sizes, colours and metallic finishes.

Left The use of open fires need not be limited to traditional interiors. For this flat the architects designed a compact and graphic fireplace to hold a stylish steel basket with gas-fired coals.

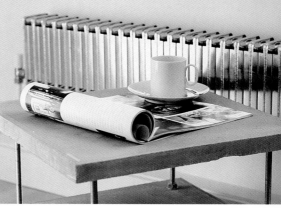

Top An elegant finned tube radiator was the perfect choice in this unusually shaped attic bedroom. It fits perfectly into the small vertical space created where the floor meets the pitch of the roof.

Above A floor-mounted convector radiator has a smart and shiny modern design. These radiators can be purchased by length, depending on just how much warmth is required to heat your particular space.

LIGHTING

All too often lighting is only an afterthought, when it should be an important consideration from the outset. Effective lighting doesn't just cater for your functional needs, it makes the most of the aesthetics of a room, bringing life to colours in, highlighting interesting architectural details, features and textures, and lending atmosphere to a space.

Pace the lighting in your home to create a variety of light levels for different functions. Built-in and recessed ceiling fittings produce good general and background illumination – they need to be installed before you decorate to cause the least disruption. They are a neat alternative to traditional overhead fittings in small spaces since they don't intrude as much, and illuminating a whole area opens it up and makes it appear larger. Recessed fittings can be angled to illuminate architectural features or paintings and also work well if positioned on staircase walls just above the treads.

Inexpensive fluorescent tubes concealed at the top of a bookcase framework or shelving unit throw out a good level of light, and they provide the right worktop illumination when fitted under kitchen wall cupboards. When lighting is fitted on a ceiling, with a screen below that does not cover the whole area, light washes out from the edges and floods the ceiling, making it appear higher than it really is.

Right Neat and precise squares of light, recessed into the lower part of this staircase wall, illuminate the treads for safety and accent the warm tones of the natural wood stairs and the cinnamon-coloured walls.

Far right Several types of lighting working together create an interesting vista. Recessed ceiling fittings are directed to illuminate paintings on the wall, and recessed floor fittings throw light up and around the wood-lined walls and ceiling, accentuating the effect of a tunnel leading to a brighter area.

DIRECTORY

ARCHITECTS AND DESIGNERS

AEM Studio Ltd
80 O'Donnell Court
Brunswick Centre
Brunswick Square
London WC1N 1NX
T 020 7713 9191
F 020 7713 9199
pages 8, 9, 19, 20, 21,
46, 47, 76, 94l, 101r, 105,
116l

Ash Sakula Architects
Studio 115
38 Mount Pleasant
London WC1X 0AN
T 020 7837 9735
F 020 7837 9708
pages 31, 40, 41, 65,
69, 97l, 101l, 110,
111r, 112r

Circus Architects
1 Summer's Street
London EC1R 5BD
T 020 7833 1888
F 020 7833 1888
pages 7, 14, 15, 16, 17,
37, 56, 57, 78, 79, 92,
93, 100r, 109, 119l

Granit Chartered
Architects
112 Battersea
Business Centre
Lavender Hill
London SW11 5QL
T 020 7924 4555
F 020 7924 5666
pages 13, 22, 24, 25,
42, 43 61, 71, 80, 81,
98r, 100l, 117t

Hawkins Brown
Architects
60 Bastwick Street
London EC1V 3JN
T 020 7336 8030
F 020 7336 8851
pages 32, 33, 34, 35,
88, 89

Hugh Broughton
Architects
4 Addison Bridge Place
London W14 8XP
T 020 7602 8840
F 020 7602 5254
pages 2, 10, 11, 96,
106, 107

Hugh Pilkington
Architect
Richmond House
Gedgrave
Orford
Suffolk IP12 2BU
T 01394 450102
page 120

Littman Goddard
Hogarth
12 Chelsea Wharf
15 Lots Road
London SW10 0QJ
T 020 7351 7871
F 020 7351 4110
pages 38, 39, 54, 55,
66, 67, 72, 73, 77, 87,
98m, 117b

Wells Mackereth
Architects
Unit 14
Archer Street Studios
10–11 Archer Street
London W1V 7HG
T 020 7287 5504
F 020 7287 5506
pages 27, 28, 29, 48, 49,
62, 90, 91, 98l, 99, 103,
112l, 115, 116r, 121.

The Works
T 01502 578793
page 63

FURNITURE, STORAGE AND ACCESSORIES

Aero
347–349 Kings Road
London SW3 5ES
T 020 7351 0511
F 020 7351 0522

The Conran Shop
Michelin House
81 Fulham Road
London SW3 6RD
T 020 7589 7401
F 020 7823 7015

Divertimenti
139 Fulham Road
London SW3 6SD
T 020 7581 8065
F 020 7823 9429

The Futon Company
169 Tottenham
Court Road
London W1P 9LH
T 020 7636 9984
F 020 7383 3296

Habitat
The Heals Building
196 Tottenham
Court Road
London W1P 9LD
(for nearest branch)
T 0845 6010740

Heals
The Heals Builiding
196 Tottenham
Court Road
London W1P 9LD
T 020 7636 1666
F 020 7436 5129

The Holding Company
243–245 Kings Road
London SW3 5EL
T 020 7352 1600
F 020 7352 7495

Ikea
255 North
Circular Road
Neasden
London NW10 0GQ
(for nearest branch)
T 020 8208 5600

The Inventory
10 Harbour Parade
West Quay
Southampton
Hampshire
SO15 1BA
T 01703 336141
F 01703 336198

Lakeland Ltd
Alexandra Buildings
Windermere
Cumbria LA23 1BQ
(for nearest branch)
T 015394 88100

Muji
157 Kensington
High Street
London W8 6SU
T 020 7376 2484
F 020 7938 3665

Oggetti
133/143 Fulham Road
London SW3 6RT
T 020 7581 8088
F 020 7581 8244

Purves & Purves
80–81/83 Tottenham
Court Road
London W1P 9HD
T 020 7580 8223
F 020 7580 8244

SCP
135–139 Curtain Road
London EC2A 3BX
T 020 7739 1869
F 020 7729 4224

The Shaker Shop
25 Harcourt Street
London W1 1DT
T 020 7724 7672
F 020 7724 6640

LIGHTING
Anglepoise
Enfield Industrial Estate
Redditch
Worcestershire
B97 6DR
(for nearest stockist)
T 01527 63771

Artemide
106 Great Russell Street
London WC1B 3LI
(for nearest stockist)
T 020 7631 5200

Concord Lighting
174 High Holborn
London WC1V 7AA
T 020 7497 1400
F 020 7497 1404

Flos Ltd UK
31 Lisson Grove
London NW1 6UV
(for nearest stockist)
T 020 7258 0600

Mr Light
275 Fulham Road
London SW10 9PZ
T 020 7351 1487
F 020 7351 3484

**BATHROOMS
& KITCHENS**
CP Hart
Newham Terrace
Hercules Road
London SE1 7DR
T 020 7902 1000
F 020 7902 1001

BATHROOMS
Ideal Standard
The Bathroom Works
National Avenue
Kingston-upon-Hull
Humberside HU5 4HS
T 01482 346461
F 01482 445886

KITCHENS
Bulthaup
37 Wigmore Street
London W1H 9LD
T 020 7495 3663
F 020 7495 0139

**FOLDAWAY BEDS
& SPECIALIST
FITTINGS FOR
CUPBOARDS**

Hafele UK Limited
Swift Valley
Industrial Estate
Rugby
Warwickshire
CV21 1RD
(for nearest stockist)
T 01788 542020

**RADIATORS
& HEATING**

Bisque Radiators
15 Kingsmead Square
Bath
Banes BA1 2AE
(for nearest stockist)
T 01225 469244

Clyde Combustions Ltd
Cox Lane
Chessington
Surrey KT9 1SL
(for nearest stockist)
T 020 8391 2020

Faral Radiators
Tropical House
Charlwoods Road
East Grinstead
West Sussex RH19 2HJ
T 01342 315757
F 01342 315362

Hudevad Britain
Bridge House
Bridge Street
Walton-on-Thames
Surrey KT12 1AL
(for nearest stockist)
T 01932 247835

Mysson Heating
Somerdon Road
Hull
Yorkshire HU9 5PE
T 01482 711709
F 01482 787221

Smiths Environmental
Products
4–7A Blackall
Industrial Estate
Chelmsford
Essex CM3 5UW
T 01245 324900
F 01245 324422

**UNDERFLOOR
HEATING**

David Robbens
Heating Systems
Old Farewood Lane
Crowhurst
East Sussex TN33 9AE
T 0800 454 569
F 01424 830 160

Ippec Systems
66 Rea Street South
Birmingham
West Midlands B5 6B5
T 0121 622 4333
F 0121 622 5768

Kee Radiant
Floor Heating
Unit 7
Scarborough Road
Industrial Estate
Banbridge
County Down
Ireland BT32 3QG
T 018206 24141
F 018206 28358

Nu-Heat UK
Unit 5
Lakes Court
Old Fore Street
Sidmouth
Devon EX10 8LP
T 01395 578482
F 01395 515502

**HIT AND MISS
STAIRCASE**

J&R Fabrication
Unit 6A1
Caxton Trading Estate
Printing House Lane
Hayes
Middlesex UB3 1BE
T 020 8569 0129
F 020 8569 0139

INDEX

Page references in **bold** refer to illustrations

audio equipment **20**, 21, **48**, 106, **107**

basins 17, 96–9
bathrooms 7
  basins 17, 96–9
  baths 17, 94–5
  decorating ideas 89, **102**, 103
  display ideas **102**, 103
  fittings 17, 89, **92**, 94–101
  on galleries 28, **29**, 36, **37**, **42–3**, **94**, 95
  lavatories 17, 100–1
  lighting **90–1**, **92**, **93**, **94**, 95, 96, **97**
  plumbing **88**, 89, 96, 99, 100, **101**, **102**, 103
  showers 92–3, 95
  storage space 17, **94**, 95, **96**, **97**, **98**, **99**
  taps 89, **96**, 98–9
baths 17, 94–5
bedrooms see sleeping areas
beds
  folding 7, **8–9**, 36, **37**, 44, **72–3**, 74, 106
  raised **8–9**, **14–15**, 16, **17**, **46**, 74, **75**, 77
  screening 74

beds cont
  size 77–8
  with storage space 11, **77**, 81
blinds **10**, 16, **106**
books 36, **42**, **44**, 59, 106, **107**, **112**, 113
brick 21, **22**, 24

CDs **43**, **48**, 106, **107**
ceilings **10–11**, **24–5**, **33**, 44, 118
chairs 35, 113
clutter 7, 36, 43–4, 56, 59, 64–6, 85
colour
  for balance 21, **28–9**, **108**, 109
  and lighting 82
  mood creation **92**
  for space creation **8–9**, **10–11**, 39, 60, 82, **88**, 89
  strong **38**, 39, **56–7**, 60, **61**, 82
  for zoning 17, **38–41**, **56–7**, 60–3, **76**, 77, **82–3**, **100**
concrete 40, **62**, 63
convertibility 6, **7**, **54–5**, 72–4, 106, 109
cookers 25, **57**, 65
cooking equipment **52**, 56, **58**, 59, 60, **61**, 64–5, **66**
corridors 6, 106
crockery 56, **59**, 60, **61**, 64, 65, 66

cupboards
  for bathroom fittings **97**, 99, **100**
  built-in **48**, 56, 78
  for kitchen appliances **53**, 56, **57**
  mirrored **98**, **99**
  for spare beds 7
  for washing appliances 23, **24**, **102**, 103, **120**, **121**
  as window seats 60, **61**

decorating ideas 39–41, 60–3, **78–9**, **82–3**, 89, 102–3
desks 28, **29**, **108**, 109, **112**–13
dining areas
  with beds 36, **37**
  convertibility 6, **7**, **54–5**
  in kitchens **64**, 65
  in living areas 7, 32, **54–5**
dishwashers 25
display ideas 57–9, 66–9, **84**, 85, **102**, 103
doors
  folding **10**
  glass **20**, 21, **29**, 72, **73**, **90–1**
  sliding **20**, 21, 26, **27**, **38–9**, 92, **112**, 113
  wooden 24

electrical equipment 35, 36, **48**, **57**, 65

floor levels 7, 36, **37**, **56–7**
floorplans 17, **20**, 25, **29**
food storage **53**, 54, 55, 66
freezers 17
fridges 17, **25**, 53, 54

galleries
  with bathrooms 28, **29**, 36, **37**, **42–3**, **94**, 95
  as design feature 11, **22**, 23, 44
  for sleeping 11, 36, **37**, **42–3**, 74–5, 77
  as storage space 11, 26, **27**, 28, 77
  as working areas 11, 24, **25**, 36, **37**, 44, **108**, 109
glass
  ceilings **33**
  doors **20**, 21, **29**, 72, **73**, **90–1**
  panels **20–1**, 36, **37**, **38–9**, **76**, 77, **79**, 92
  partitions 48
  roofs 40, **41**, **42–3**, 44
  sandblasted 48
  shelving 21, **102**, 103
  in showers **90–1**, 92–3
  stained 96, **97**
  tiles **16–17**, 92, **93**, **100**
  walls 19, **20**, 21, **33**, **65**, 92, **93**, **100**
  see also mirrors
granite **56**, 63

hallways 6, **25**, 28, **29**, 106
hanging racks 69
heating 116–17
hi-fi equipment see audio equipment

kitchens
  clutter 56, 59, 64–6
  decorating ideas 60–3
  dining areas **64**, 65
  display ideas 57–9, 66–9
  lighting **58**, 59, **65**, 66, 69
  screening **10**, **16–17**, **20–1**, 44, **45**, 53
  sinks 53
  storage space 17, **28–9**, 52–4, **56–9**, 60, **61**, 65

ladders **28–9**, 122
laundry areas 23, **25**, 28, 29, **120–1**
lavatories 17, 100–1
lighting
  adapting 118–19
  ambient 48, 110
  bathrooms **90–1**, 92, **93**, **94**, 95, 96, **97**
  bedrooms 72, **76**, 77, **79**, 81, 82–3
  and colour 82
  to create space 47, 48
  fluorescent **18–19**, **66**, 118
  enhanced by glass 7, **16–17**, 19, 21, **33**
  importance of 118

lighting cont
  kitchens **58**, 59, **65**, 66, 69
  living areas **42**, 44, **45**, 47, 48
  enhanced by mirrors 81, 82, **83**, 92, 93
  natural **18–19**, 21, **64**, 65, 66, 110
  recessed **90–1**, **112**, 113, 118, **119**
  shelves 66, **102**, 118
  task 35, 48, 110, 111, **112**, **113**
  in working areas 110–11, **112**, 113
living areas
  with bedrooms 72–4
  convertibility 7
  decorating ideas **39–41**
  as dining areas 7, 32, **54–5**
  lighting **42**, 44, **45**, 47, 48
  storage space 36, 43

marble 63, **84**, 85, **94**, 95
materials
  for balance **22**, 24
  in bathrooms 89
  in kitchens **62**, 63
  patterned 40, **41**
  for space creation **10–11**, 16, 21, 74, **75**
  textured 40
  for zoning 40
  see also brick; glass; metal; stainless steel

metal
    in bathrooms 96, **97**,
        103
    blinds **10**, **106**
    shelves 66, **68**, 69
    staircases **8–9**, **16**,
        22
    worktops **68**, 69
    see also stainless steel
mezzanines see galleries
microwaves 53, 56, **57**
mirrors
    on cupboards **98**, **99**
    enhanced by lighting
        81, 82, **83**, 92, **93**
    recessed **90–1**
    as screens **7**
    in shelving 85
    for space creation 81,
        92, **93**, 103
    as walls 101

niches see recesses

paintings see pictures
panels
    glass 36, **37**, **38–9**, 76,
        77, **79**, 92, **100**
    sliding **20–1**, 28, **29**
partitions 47–8
pattern 40, **41**
pictures 36, 84, **85**
plate racks **68**, 69
plumbing
    bathroom **88**, 89,
        96, 99, 100, 101,
        102, 103
    laundry areas 121

radiators 103, 116–17
recesses
    bookshelves **44**
    for display 11, **16**
    mirrored **90–1**
    for storage 11, **44**,
        90–1, **101**, **102**, **103**
    for televisions 48, **49**
    regulations 6, 16, 45, 47
roofspace 23, 24, 44, 72,
    80, **81**, **108**, **109**, **117**

screens
    beds hidden by **7**, 20,
        38–9, 74
    as design feature **16**
    to divide space 7, 47
    kitchens hidden by **10**,
        16–17, **20–1**, 44,
        45, 53
    mirrored **7**
    workspace hidden by
        106, 109, **112**, 113
seating
    built-in **65**
    in kitchens 20, 21,
        54–5, **65**
    in living areas 35
    with storage space
        11, **94–5**
    in working areas 106,
        107, 109, 113
serving hatches 32,
    33, 55
Shaker style 69
shelves
    in bathrooms **100**,
        101, **102**, 103

shelves cont
    bedhead 74, **78**, 81
    for display **20**, 59, 85,
        102, 103
    to divide space 36
    glass **21**, **102**, 103
    kitchen 66–9
    lighting **66**, **102**, 118
    metal 66, **68**, 69
    with mirrors 85
    open 36, **44**, 59, 60,
        61, 66–9
    recessed 11, **44**, **90–1**,
        101, **102**, **103**
    window **66–7**, **69**
showers **90–1**, 92–3, 95
shutters see panels
sinks 53, **120**
slate 63, **101**
sleeping areas
    clutter 85
    convertibility 6, 72, **73**
    decorating ideas
        78–9, **82–3**
    in dining areas 36, **37**
    display ideas **84**, 85
    furniture 77–8
    on galleries 11, 36,
        37, **42–3**, 74–5, 77
    lighting 72, **76**, 77, **79**,
        81, 82–3
    in living areas 72–4
    screening 20, **38–9**, 74
    storage space 77–8, 81,
        82, **83**
    as working areas 72,
        106, 109
sofas **29**, 35, 43–4

spare rooms 6, **7**, 36, 37
stainless steel
    in bathrooms 96, **97**,
        103
    in kitchens 26, 28,
        62, 63
    in living areas 40
staircases **22**, 23, 24
stairs
    as design feature
        23, **33**, 40, **41**,
        46, **47**, 77
    to divide space **47**
    lighting 118, **119**
    metal **8–9**, **16**
    understair storage
        8–9, 11, 122
Starck, Philippe 96, 99
stone **17**, 40, 63
stools 44
storage space
    audio equipment
        20, 21, 48, 106, **107**
    bathroom 17, **94**, 95,
        96, **97**, **98**, **99**
    for books 36, **42**, **44**,
        106, **107**, **112**, 113
    built-in **43–4**, **48**, 56, 78
    CDs **43**, **48**, 106, **107**
    for clutter 7, 36, **43–4**,
        64–6
    electrical equipment
        36, **48**, **57**
    food **53**, 54, 55, 66
    on galleries 11, 26, **27**,
        28, 77
    kitchen 17, **28–9**, 52–4,
        56–9, 60, **61**, 65

storage space cont
    in living areas 36, 43
    overspill 122–3
    in sleeping areas 77–8,
        81, 82, **83**
    understairs **8–9**, 11,
        122
    wall 7, **10–11**, 21,
        122, **123**
structural alterations 18,
    44, 46, 77

tables 6, **28**, 32, 43, 54–5
taps 89, **94**, 95, **96**, 98–9
televisions
    recessed 48, **49**
    seating for 35
    on storage units **20**,
        21, 26, **27**, 28, 60, **61**
tiles **16–17**, **22**, 24,
    90–1, 92, **93**, **100**
towel rails 96, **97**, 98, 103
tumble driers **24**, 121

understair storage **8–9**,
    11, 122
utility areas see laundry
    areas

walls
    glass 19, **20**, 21, **33**, **65**,
        93, **100**
    mirrored **101**
    as storage space 7,
        10–11, 21, **26**, 28,
        53, 122, **123**
    with workspace **108**,
        109

washing machines **24**,
    102, 103, 121
WCs **17**, 100–1
windows **25**, **66–7**, 69
wood
    doors 24
    floors **8–9**, 16, 21,
        22, 23, 24, 40
    in kitchens **58**, 59, 63
    lighting **118–19**
    for space creation 16
    walls 44, **45**, **102**, 103,
        108, 109
working areas
    in bedrooms 72
    case study 26–9
    convertibility 6
    decorating ideas **108**,
        109
    desks 28, **29**, **108**,
        109, 112–13
    on galleries 11, 24, **25**,
        36, **37**, 44, **108**, 109
    lighting **110–11**, **112**,
        113
    professional 106, 109,
        112, 113
    screening **10**, 106, 109,
        112, 113
    in sleeping areas 106,
        109
    small 106, **108**, 109
    storage space **108**, 109
    worktops 23, 53–4, **58**,
        59, 63, 65, **68**, 69

Author's acknowledgments

My thanks for their help and enthusiasm in finding locations for this book go especially to the following architects: Pascal Madoc Jones and Glyn Emrys at AEM Studio Ltd; Cany Ash at Ash Sakula Architects; Joanna Mehan at Granit Chartered Architects; Sally Mackereth at Wells Mackereth Architects; Vicky Emmett at Hawkins Brown Architects; Ian Hogarth at Littman Goddard Hogarth; Donnathea Bradford at Circus Architects. Thanks to all of the owners who allowed us to photograph their homes, especially Andrea Spencer, Pat Walker and Roger Hipwell, and Linda Farrow and Charlie Hawkins at The Works. Thanks also for excellent advice on use of colour to Judy Smith, Colour Consultant at Crown Paints, and for bathroom advice to Louis Saliman at CP Hart. The author would also like to thank Judith More, Janis Utton and Stephen Guise at Mitchell Beazley for most welcome encouragement, help and patience. Finally, a huge thank you to Dominic Blackmore for helping to find the locations and for taking such splendid photographs.